Religious Demography of India

Religious Demography of India

Myths and Realities

Edited by

Lancy Lobo
Jayesh Shah

RAWAT PUBLICATIONS
Jaipur • New Delhi • Bangalore • Guwahati • Kolkata

ISBN 978-81-316-0932-3

Published by
Prem Rawat for **Rawat Publications**
Satyam Apts, Sector 3, Jawahar Nagar, Jaipur 302 004 (India)
Phone: 0141 265 1748 / 7006 Fax: 0141 265 1748
E-mail: info@rawatbooks.com
Website: www.rawatbooks.com

New Delhi Office
4858/24, Ansari Road, Daryaganj, New Delhi 110 002
Phone: 011 2326 3290

Also at *Bangalore, Guwahati* and *Kolkata*

Typeset by Rawat Computers, Jaipur

Printed at Chaman Enterprises, New Delhi

Contents

List of Figures

List of Tables

Abbreviations

BJP	Bharatiya Janata Party
CPR	Contraceptive Prevalence Rate
DPT	Dynamic Trunking Protocol
EPW	*Economic and Political Weekly*
IIPS	International Institute for Population Sciences
KVP	Kandhamal Vikas Parishad
NDA	National Democratic Alliance
NFHS	National Family Health Survey
NSSO	National Sample Survey Office
OBC	Other Backward Class
PIB	Press Information Bureau
PIL	Public Interest Litigation
PKJS	Phulbani Kui Jana Kalyana Sangha
PKSS	Phulbani Kui Samanya Samiti
RSS	Rashtriya Swayamsevak Sangh
SC	Scheduled Caste
ST	Scheduled Tribe
TFR	Total Fertility Rate
VHP	Vishva Hindu Parishad
ZYNG	Zoroastrian Youth for the Next Generation

Glossary

Ahura Mazda	wise Lord
Artha	economy/ wealth
Beti	unpaid labour
Dharma	religion
Ghar Wapsi	home coming (reconversion)
Go Raksha Andolana	campaign against cow slaughter
Hata	weekly market
Jagruti	awareness
Jajmani	a system of relationship between caste within a village
Kama	love, erotic love, desire
Kumbhar	potter
Logos spermatikos	seed-bearing word
Lohar	blacksmith
Love jihad	Muslims wooing Hindu girls in marriage
Mita	ritual friend
Nama Sankirtana	devotional or religious songs
Paganus	village idiot

Paravartana	reconversion
Relegere	re-trace; re-read
Religio	religion
Sampradaya	tradition/denomination
sanatana dharma	eternal religion
Sangathan	organisation
Sastra	scriptures
Siva Mandir	Siva temple
Swadeshi	indigenous
Swaraj	self-rule, self-government, home rule
Vanvas	time spent in the forest
Videshi	foreign
Zamindar	landlord

Acknowledgements

Pluralism has been tested from time to time and increasingly so over the years in India. Use and abuse of religious demography has been on the rise over the decades for religion based identity politics. The Centre for Culture and Development (CCD) Vadodara, organized a national seminar on the 'Religious demography of India' and invited papers from renowned scholars from different fields. This volume brings together select papers of the seminar. We are indeed grateful to the former editor of three national dailies, as also the former member of Rajya Sabha, Shri H.K. Dua for giving the Foreword to this volume. Professors A.M. Shah and J.S. Bandukwala have given their valuable time and guidance; Amba Gamit and her team prepared the manuscript and special thanks are due to Rawat Publications for their enthusiastic response in taking up this volume to the press.

Lancy Lobo
Jayesh Shah

Contributors

J.S. Bandukwala, Retired Professor M.S. University, Baroda and former PUCL chairperson of Gujarat.

R.B. Bhagat, Professor, Department of Migration and Urban Studies, International Institute for Population Sciences, Mumbai.

H.K. Dua, Eminent Editor of three national dailies (*Indian Express, Hindustan Times* and *Tribune*) as well as former member of the Rajya Sabha.

Meher Singh Gill, Former Professor, Department of Geography, Punjabi University, Patiala, Punjab.

Lancy Lobo, Director, Centre for Culture and Development, Vadodara.

Himanshu Sekhar Mishra, Assistant Professor, Political Science Department, Sambalpur University, Orissa.

Ambrose Pinto, Former Executive Director of Indian Social Institute and currently Principal of St. Aloysius College, Bangalore.

Jayesh Shah, Research Consultant, Centre for Culture and Development, Vadodara.

U.V. Somayajulu, CEO and Executive Director, Sigma Research and Consulting, New Delhi.

Sebastian Vazapilly teaches at Gujarat Vidya Deep, Sevasi, Vadodara.

Leela Visaria, Retired Professor, Gujarat Institute of Development Research, Ahmedabad.

Foreword

Pluralism Is India's Strength: Let's Not Fritter It Away

H.K. Dua

The idea of 'pluralism' has a symbiotic relationship with the idea of India. Neither can survive without the other. Unless the two streams of thought flow together and at some point down the line embrace each other, this nation of over a billion people will be in trouble.

Those who fought for freedom under Mahatma Gandhi's leadership and many others understood the importance of pluralism for national unity which was badly needed after the British raj ended. It was essential for building a new India. It is still needed.

The Constitution our Founding Fathers came out with represented a kind of national consensus that underlined the importance of a plural society and a plural polity for an independent India.

Most debates in the Constituent Assembly reflected this national consensus, notwithstanding widespread communal riots and travails of the partition. The Indian National Congress and most other parties underlined the importance of the idea of a plural and democratic society and polity. The consensus, with various ups and downs, has come to grow during nearly seven decades since independence and after the adoption of the Constitution.

Lately, voices, however, are being raised by influential people in different parts of the country questioning this consensus. Not only these voices are in effect questioning this national consensus but these are even challenging the basis of the Constitution. This is unfortunate and risky in the long run.

Critics of the constitutional scheme point out that the world 'secular' was inserted in the Preamble of the Constitution only in 1976 during the Emergency. Their argument is flawed and does not shake the basis on which the entire constitutional scheme has evolved.

Not only in the Preamble, but elsewhere also the Constitution underlines the principle of secularism in one form or another, and what secularism or pluralism really mean in the Indian context. Challenging the constitutional scheme on the ground that the word 'secularism' was added later does not invalidate the entire constitutional scheme which stands on secular and democratic principle.

India is a diverse country, yet over the centuries it has survived as a nation, if not as a nation state which is of a recent origin in political and territorial terms. The essence of Indian nation incorporates the idea of oneness of India, despite the diversity of the social, cultural and political fabric of India encompassing hundreds of castes, several religions, languages and regional variations. These divisions in the Indian mosaic is viewed by positive and forward-looking thinkers as a sort of unity in diversity.

Looked otherwise, these have often proved divisive. Lately, the concept of unity in diversity is being challenged by those who tend to believe that India belongs to one dominant majority religion, which at best may or may not accommodate those who are minorities in their reckoning. This kind of thinking is retrograde and certainly does not reflect a forward-looking mindset.

Justifying caste divides as our heritage to be proud of is unhealthy, and perhaps meant to serve the interest of dominant upper caste. Also, sharp is the gender divide. Regarding women as weaker sex and not as equal citizens of the land reflects discriminatory and archaic thinking, meant to prevent half of our population from contributing to nation-building. Looking selectively back into history and destroying a mosque has not strengthened the idea of a tolerant India but worked against the very concept. The Khap Panchayats' sitting in judgement on the rights of young men and women, as also the so-called honour killings, is against the rule of law, and abhorrent. Discrimination against dalits is still continuing in many parts of the land despite constitutional guarantees. The anger of the tribals, who are 8 per cent of the population, is leading to Maoist insurgency in Jharkhand and Chhattisgarh and several other areas. The policymakers need to remember that social, political and economic tensions that are developing under the surface and above have to be managed urgently.

Alienation of the various sections of the society, whatever the factors such as religion, region, language and caste or gender, from the mainstream leads to anger and in turn to socio-politico disaffection. Whatever the deeper causes, sectoral alienation and anger sharpen social and political divide – pushing back the idea of oneness.

Intolerance to dissent also slows down the evolution of a plural polity. Every citizen or a section of society has the right to free expression and the majority have a duty to listen. Tolerance, a spirit of accommodation, listening to inconvenient truths and a spirit of reconciliation are important for creating a new India – a liberal, inclusive and plural democracy where the 'loneliest and the lost' can hold his or her head high.

India has to be strong – and would require collective will and effort to be so – where every citizen, irrespective of caste, creed and religion, man or woman, rich or poor, will have to lend shoulder to the building of a new India. This would also require broader mindsets, capacity to listen to others' opinion, even if it is contrarian or a dissenting view. Dissenting opinion is in nation's interest. It should not be drowned out, branding it as anti-nation.

A plural polity requires a liberal and plural approach to governance. The executive's administration should not be encouraged to be partial towards the majority, but be neutral while discharging its legitimate duty. The people's faith in the administration will grow if it can earn the trust of the entire people, particularly of those who are often ignored and kept out of the pale. Alienation of a section of people causes heart burning and anger and encourages a non-participative climate further weakening harmony and national unity. The 'they-and-us' approach will always work against liberal, pluralistic and democratic India. Unchecked, the sociopolitical divides will further corrode unity and national harmony.

1 Introduction

Lancy Lobo and Jayesh Shah

The differential growth rates of religious communities is a sensitive issue that can be easily exploited for fomenting passions based on prejudices by different stakeholders. Religion is something that should create harmony, peace in a country or in a region, but on the contrary it has become a divisive force creating conflicts and tensions, not only in India but also at the international level. Such type of religious conflicts, tensions and intolerance are threats to democracy in India and also a threat to the world peace at global level. Many demographers have warned the world about the issue of migration of refugees and its impact on demography and democratic practices.

Based on the religious composition, India's population is subdivided into Buddhists, Christians, Hindus, Jains, Muslims, Sikhs and '*Other*' religious group, which includes Parsis, Jewish, tribal religions and so on. Further, in every census the Registrar General and Census Commissioner of India customarily present another category of population called *Religion not stated*. Many historians, demographers and social scientists generally show their interest in studying only the first six categories of religion as stated above, because almost 99 per cent of the total population of India falls into one of these six categories. These six religions are recognized as *Major Religious Groups* of India.

According to the 2011 census, in terms of numbers, Hindus occupy the first position (79.8%), Muslims occupy the second (14.2%), Christians occupy the third (02.3%) and then Sikhs (01.7%), Buddhists (00.7%) and Jains (00.4%) take the fourth, fifth and sixth, respectively. However, Muslims, Christians, Sikhs, Buddhists and Parsi (Zoroastrian) communities are declared as *Minority Religious Groups* as per National Commission for Minority Act 1992. These groups constitute less than 20 per cent (Murthy and Ram 2010) of India's population. Figure 1.1 (http://indianexpress.com) shows some basic facts about religion and population for 1991, 2001 and 2011.

Given that the population growth rate by religion is a sensitive issue and easily exploited for fomenting passions based on prejudices, it is not known why the census released the unadjusted growth rates (Raghuraman 2004: 1). The census 2001 provided an opportunity to analyse and understand nearly 1,700 religious groups which were recorded in earlier censuses and codified in the 2001 census (Bhagat 2004: 4292–93). Here the question also arises about how the religion of tribal communities has been shown in census. Many tribals have been counted as Hindu. It will be interesting to verify on this perspective. This provides an enormous opportunity to understand India's religious and cultural diversity, if unpublished data are also made available to the concerned users.

Although the proportions of *Other* (00.7% in 2011 census) are too low to matter demographically, they are still important to understand the diversity of religious faiths in India. On the other hand, the numerical dominance of religious groups is so strong that India is ultimately projected as a country of two main religious groups, namely Hindus as majority (966.2 million comprising 79.8 per cent of the total as per 2011 census) and Muslims as the largest minority (172.2 million constituting 14.2% of the total as per 2011 census).

Figure 1.1 *Some Basic Facts about Religion and Population*

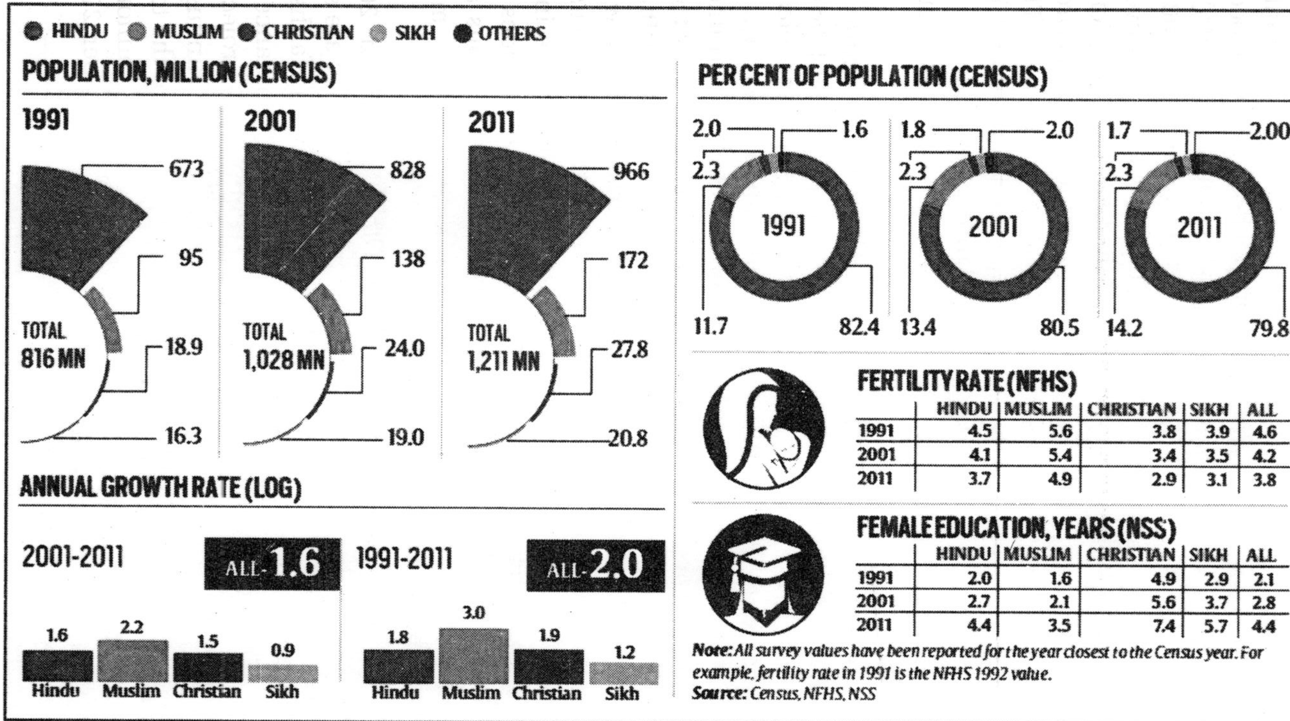

FERTILITY RATE (NFHS)

	HINDU	MUSLIM	CHRISTIAN	SIKH	ALL
1991	4.5	5.6	3.8	3.9	4.6
2001	4.1	5.4	3.4	3.5	4.2
2011	3.7	4.9	2.9	3.1	3.8

FEMALE EDUCATION, YEARS (NSS)

	HINDU	MUSLIM	CHRISTIAN	SIKH	ALL
1991	2.0	1.6	4.9	2.9	2.1
2001	2.7	2.1	5.6	3.7	2.8
2011	4.4	3.5	7.4	5.7	4.4

Note: *All survey values have been reported for the year closest to the Census year. For example, fertility rate in 1991 is the NFHS 1992 value.*
Source: *Census, NFHS, NSS*

I

In the census year 1901, Hindus accounted for 194 million and Muslims accounted for only 29.9 million. Christians, Sikhs, Buddhists and Jains accounted for 2.6 million, 1.7 million, 1.3 million and 0.1 million, respectively. When compared to Hindus, Muslims and Christians, the numerical strength displayed by other religious groups seem to be negligible, for India. In the census year 2001, Hindus accounted for 827.6 million and Muslims accounted for 138.2 million. Christians, Sikhs, Buddhists and Jains accounted for 24.1 million, 19.2 million, 8.0 million and 4.2 million, respectively.

In absolute terms, over the past 100 years, while the number of Hindus increased by 633.6 million, Muslims increased by 108.3 million and Christians and Sikhs increased to 21.4 million and 17.6 million, respectively, while Buddhists and Jains increased by 7.8 million and 2.9 million, respectively.

The proportional growth of Muslims is increasing over the years, successively and relatively, compared to all other religions of India. The proportion of Hindus has declined from 83.5 per cent in the year 1961 to 79.8 per cent by the year 2011, thus showing a decline of 03.7 per cent points. On the contrary, the proportion of Muslims has increased from 10.7 per cent in 1961 to 14.2 per cent in the year 2011, showing an increase of 03.5 per cent points during this period. Although the exponential growth rate of Muslims is higher than any other religions in India, the growth rate of all major religious communities is showing a declining trend. The growth rate of the Jains is the lowest.

The differential growth rates of religious communities have been an issue. There has been a time lag in the adoption of family planning and consequently the onset of fertility decline among various religious communities. The issue of immigration is also a political subject. At the same time different states in India are getting co-religionists from the neighbouring countries such as Bangladesh by means of immigration (Premi 2004: 4297–302). Data on outmigration by Hindus from India to other countries between 1901 and 2001 can also throw light on the declining growth rate of Hindus. However, the same may also be considered whether the declining proportion of Christians in Goa is the result of outmigration?

Demographic Issues and Hindu–Muslim Polarization

A census is not only a passive exercise of counting people, but is also actively engaged in capturing reality through categories and their definitions. Categories are also the outcome of the perceptions of census officials, their earlier experience in dealing with such categories or a negotiated outcome with those confronted in the counting (Jones 1981: 73–102). The categorization of religious and ethnic communities and their enumeration have deep social and political impacts in India. We find that the very syndrome of majority and minority in religious terms was less known, but was made through the conscious census exercises that began in the late nineteenth century (Das 1994). After the census, numbers became a political tool as Hindus came to know that they constituted a majority (Bhagat 2013: 434–48).

The beginning of the census also coincided with the electoral process first started in municipal bodies and later in legislative assemblies during British rule. This raised the importance of the figures of religion in seeking representation for the various religious communities in the emerging political institutions (Census of India 1931). The colonial census data also sparked off communal debates on the size and growth of population of different religious communities. The Hindu population had a substantially low growth rate between 1891 and 1901, and even declined between 1911 and 1921. The low growth rate or decline in the Hindu population created turbulence in the relationship between Hindus and Muslims (Bhagat 2013: 434–48).

On the basis of figures from the 1901 census, Mukherji (1909) drew attention towards the declining proportion of Hindus in the total population. He also stirred up fears of Hindus being swallowed up in the next 420 years and convinced Swami Shraddhanand, a prominent Hindu leader, to take up the work of re-conversion from Mohammedan and Christians to Hinduism. Swami Shraddhanand, alarmed by the growth of Muslim population, also wrote an influential book entitled '*Hindu Sangathan: Saviour of Dying Race*' in 1926 (Shraddhanand 1926). Thus, the idea of demographic decline became a core feature of Hindu communalism in later years.

The demographic anxiety about Hindus being outnumbered continued in independent India. Such anxiety is expressed more in view of the nature of electoral politics in the country (Prakash 1979). A book by Joshi, Bajaj and Srinivas made this point, and tried to estimate the proportion of Muslim and Christian population vis-à-vis *Indian religionists*, raising fears about Hindus turning into a minority in South Asia by the mid twenty-first century, in spite of the fact that several demographers have refuted such assertions (Joshi, Srinivas and Bajaj 2005).

Based on a study of population growth differentials between Hindus and Muslims from 1951 to 1971, Visaria observed that, 'even if the differentials in the rate of growth of Hindus and Muslims persist, India will not become a Muslim-majority nation for centuries to come. Further, the differentials observed so far most unlikely to continue in future (1974: 361–74). In another study, Bhatia concluded that there is no sound reason to believe that Muslims will become the majority community in India (1990: 121–9). Based on the differentials of Hindu–Muslim growth rates, the highest ever recorded between 1981 and 1991, Kulkarni estimated that if the observed differentials in Hindu–Muslim growth rates continue in the future, it would take about 250 years for the Muslim population to catch up with the Hindu population numerically, let alone become a majority (1996).

According to the latest report released by Pew Research Center in United States in April 2015, Hindus are projected roughly to keep pace with global population growth. Although India will continue to have a Hindu majority, by 2050 it is projected to have the world's largest Muslim population, surpassing Indonesia (Pew Research Center 2015) due to slow decline in population growth among Muslims. But even after this projection for Muslim population in India, the Hindus will be 76.7 per cent of the total population of the country in the year 2050, a decrease of mere 03.1 per cent in four decades. Table 1.1 shows top ten countries with largest Hindu population for the years 2010 and 2050.

In 2050, Muslims will be 18.4 per cent of the total population of India which is 14.2 per cent as per census 2011. As per projection of Pew Research Center, Muslims in India will be increased by 04.2 per cent in four decades. According to the projections, Hindus in India will decrease by 03.1 per cent against the increase of Muslims in India by 04.2 per cent. Table 1.2 shows top ten countries with largest Muslim population for the years 2010 and 2050.

As per census 2011, 96.6 crores are Hindus in India, while 17.2 crores are Muslims in India. Projection by Pew Research Center for the year 2050 suggests that Hindus will reach to 129.79 crores, while Muslims will reach to 31.06 crores. If we analyse census 2011 and Pew Research Center's projection for 2050, we can say that Hindus will increase by 33.19 crores, while Muslims will go up by 13.86 crores in the year 2050. We can say that though there is a slow decline in population growth among Muslims in India, the fear generated by fundamentalists that Muslims would outnumber Hindus in India, as a whole, is totally unwarranted.

Religion and Fertility

The differential growth rates of religious communities have been an issue of contest for a long time. Usually, the following causative factors are cited: (i) fertility rate and birth control, (ii) sex ratio, (iii) female education, (iv) consumption rate and the class phenomenon, (v) emigration and immigration and (vi) conversions. The practice of polygamy among Muslims is raised time and again, attributing to it their relatively higher fertility. However, the

Table 1.1 *Ten Countries with the Largest Hindu Populations, 2010 and 2050*

Sr. No.	Country	2010 Hindu Population	% of World's Hindu Population in 2010	Sr. No.	Country	2050 Hindu Population	% of World's Hindu Population in 2050
1	India	973,750,000	94.3	1	India	1,297,960,000	93.8
2	Nepal	24,170,000	2.3	2	Nepal	38,120,000	2.8
3	Bangladesh	12,680,000	1.2	3	Bangladesh	14,470,000	1.0
4	Indonesia	4,050,000	0.4	4	Pakistan	5,630,000	0.4
5	Pakistan	3,330,000	0.3	5	United States	4,780,000	0.3
6	Sri Lanka	2,830,000	0.3	6	Indonesia	4,150,000	0.3
7	United States	1,790,000	0.2	7	Sri Lanka	3,430,000	0.2
8	Malaysia	1,720,000	0.2	8	Malaysia	2,270,000	0.2
9	United Kingdom	890,000	<0.1	9	United Kingdom	1,370,000	<0.1
10	Burma (Myanmar)	820,000	<0.1	10	Canada	1,070,000	<0.1
	Subtotal	1,026,030,000	99.4		Subtotal	1,373,230,000	99.2
	Subtotal for Rest of World	6,190,000	0.6		Subtotal for Rest of World	11,120,000	0.8
	World Total	1,032,210,000	100.0		World Total	1,384,380,000	100.0

Source: Pew Research Center, April 2, 2015, 'The Future of World Religions: Population Growth Projections, 2010–2050.'

Table 1.2 *Ten Countries with the Largest Muslim Populations, 2010 and 2050*

Sr. No.	Country	2010 Muslim Population	% of World's Muslim Population in 2010	Sr. No.	Country	2050 Muslim Population	% of World's Muslim Population in 2050
1	Indonesia	209,120,000	13.1	1	India	310,660,000	11.2
2	India	176,200,000	11.0	2	Pakistan	273,110,000	9.9
3	Pakistan	167,410,000	10.5	3	Indonesia	256,820,000	9.3
4	Bangladesh	134,430,000	8.4	4	Nigeria	230,700,000	8.4
5	Nigeria	77,300,000	4.8	5	Bangladesh	182,360,000	6.6
6	Egypt	76,990,000	4.8	6	Egypt	119,530,000	4.3
7	Iran	73,570,000	4.6	7	Turkey	89,320,000	3.2
8	Turkey	71,330,000	4.5	8	Iran	86,190,000	3.1
9	Algeria	34,730,000	2.2	9	Iraq	80,190,000	2.9
10	Morocco	31,930,000	2.0	10	Afghanistan	72,190,000	2.6
	Subtotal	1,053,010,000	65.8		Subtotal	1,701,070,000	61.6
	Subtotal for Rest of World	546,700,000	34.2		Subtotal for Rest of World	1,060,410,000	38.4
	World Total	1,599,700,000	100.0		World Total	2,761,480,000	100.0

Source: Pew Research Center, April 2, 2015, 'The Future of World Religions: Population Growth Projections, 2010–2050.'

popular perception of polygamy leading to high fertility is demographically incorrect. In fact, polygamy leads to lower fertility (Basu 1997: 5–18). National Family Health Survey–2 (NFHS–2 1998–1999 and IIPS 2000) shows that only 2 per cent of women oppose the use of family planning on the ground of religion. The more recent NFHS–3 (2005–2006 and IIPS 2007) report also reiterates the fact that there is a high unmet need of family planning among currently married Muslim women (19%) compared to Hindus (12%). Furthermore, the increase in the use of modern family planning methods among Muslims was faster compared to Hindus during the two rounds of NFHS during 1992–1993 and 2005–2006.

More importantly, the differential between Hindus and Muslim fertility is not very large. The NFHS–2 shows that on average Muslim women gave birth to one child more than Hindus during 1998–1999, a rate which narrowed down to half a child during 2005–2006 as reported by NFHS–3. Further, it is important to note that between the three rounds of NFHS the fertility decline among Muslims was faster than the decline among Hindus. The total fertility rate (TFR) among Hindus declined from 3.3 to 2.8 during 1992–1993 to 1998–1999, and further to 2.6 in 2005–2006, compared to the decline from 4.4 to 3.6 and to 3.1 during the respective period among Muslims.

The faster increase in the acceptance of family planning and also the faster fertility decline among Muslims are generally glossed over in the debate of Hindu–Muslim population growth and fertility differentials that takes place after almost every census. Efforts are also made by some quarters now and then to inject demographic issues into the communal discourse and even violence (Sengupta, Kumar, and Gandevia 2003). Thus, Hindu–Muslims differentials in population growth and fertility have been a core feature of communalism since the colonial census and have continued in recent years. This sometimes is also perpetuated by academic scholars who believe in the particularized role of religion influencing higher fertility among Muslims. Such biases are harmful to communal harmony and anathema to the spread of family planning among Muslims (Bhagat 2013: 434–48). In fact, what is more likely is that universal fertility decline in the two communities will lead to eventual fertility levels that are very similar in all significant groups and sub-groups of Indian population, so that the proportional number of these groups and sub-groups also stabilize. Economic class also plays a very vital role in the fertility. Fertility of the middle class people from any religion remains almost the same. If census or NFHS or NSSO throws light on the role of economic class on fertility, it will be a value added in the data.

II

Census-Inspired 'Nationalism' Hysteria

It is an established fact that there is an illicit dramatization of misrepresented statistics of census. In a matter of such extreme and misplaced sensitivity as is routinely evoked by statistics on the growth of population by religious groups, Census of India should come out clearly with proper and correct comparison of data by religious groups. Pew Research Center (2015) also states that India will not only retain a Hindu majority but also will have the largest Muslim population of any country in the world, surpassing Indonesia by 2050.

It is true that Hindus are expected to experience a decline in their TFR over the next four decades in part because India's overall fertility rate has been dropping – from 5.9 children per woman in 1950 to 2.5 in 2010 – and is expected to fall to 1.9 by 2050. But even after this, Hindus will retain their majority. Estimates by Pew Research Center (2015) suggest that Hindus are expected to make up about 77 per cent of total population in 2050, down from about 79.5 per cent in 2011 and 80.9 per cent in 2001. Muslims will be about 18.5 per cent of total population in 2050, up from about 14.5 per cent in 2011 and about 13 per cent in 2001.

There is a much larger picture that deserves attention here. There is little in the censuses or other official data sources to provoke a reaction that is either sanguine or sanguinary (Jayaraj and Subramanian 2004: 4296–97). For the alacrity with which the misleading statistics in the recent censuses and other data sources such as Pew Research Center publication have been seized upon, and broadcast, and hammered home, serves as a remarkable contrast to the equanimity with which incalculably more pressing issues thrown up by the censuses and other data sources have been ignored (Jayaraj and Subramanian 2004: 4296–97).

These data on population have been especially 'used' to generate 'nationalism' to construct myths of 'large increase in Muslims' and perceptions of declining Hindus in numbers. This is to be noted that no major religious community in India has been declining in absolute number except Parsis. The debate relates to growth rates, and not the size of the community. Newspapers, magazines, television channels and even caste journals propounded the similar myths, with catchy titles. Such statistical formulations aided the Hindu fear of alleged numerical decline, which became much more intense in the specific context of the first decade of twenty-first century, in the context of 'Hindu *Sangathan*', 'Hindu *Jagruti*' and *Ghar Wapsi* (Gupta 2004: 4302–4). The main aim of 'nationalism', '*sangathan*' and *Ghar Wapsi* is to stop the alleged decline of Hindu numbers based on the numerical myths spread by the active media and social media.

Many of these debates can be linked to the present situation. With such arguments, even a demographic religious majority can still mentally project itself as an endangered religious group. The whole discourse is aimed at obliterating pluralism of identities, by provoking a fear of the other and propagating a constant myth of a catastrophic decline in the Hindu population (Gupta 2004: 4302–4).

Rise in Religion-based Identity Politics

Identity politics has become a prominent subject in the Indian politics in the past few years. Rise of low castes, religious identities, linguistic groups and ethnic conflicts have contributed to the significance of identity politics in India. The discourse on identity, many scholars feel, is distinctly a modern phenomenon. This is primarily a modern phenomenon because some scholars feel that emphasis on identity based on a central organizing principle of ethnicity, religion, language, gender, sexual preferences, or caste positions is a sort of 'compelling remedy for anonymity' in an otherwise impersonal modern world. Any search for an 'authentic self or identity' is not an innocent and unnuanced possibility; it involves negotiating other, often overlapping and contested, heterodox or multiple 'selves' (Brubaker 2004).

One form of identity politics is that affected through the construction of a community on the shared bond of religion. In India, numerically the Hindus are considered to be the majority, which inspires many Hindu loyalist groups such as the RSS, or the Shiv Sena and political parties such as the BJP (Bharatiya Janata Party) to claim that India is a Hindu state. These claims generate homogenizing myths about India and its history. These claims are countered by other religious groups who foresee the possibility of losing autonomy of practice of their religious and cultural life under such homogenizing claims. This initiates contestations that have often resulted in communal riots. The generally accepted myths that the identity is divided on religious lines centre on the 'appeasement theory', 'forcible religious conversions', general 'anti-Hindu' and thus 'anti-India' attitude of the minority religious groups, the 'hegemonic aspirations' of majority groups and 'denial of a sociocultural space' to minority groups.

Historically, the Hindu revivalist movement of the nineteenth century is considered to be the period that saw the demarcation of two separate cultures on religious basis – the Hindus and the Muslims that deepened further because of the partition. This division which has become institutionalized in the form of a communal ideology has become a major challenge for India's secular social fabric and democratic polity. The rise of Hindu national assertiveness, politics of representational government, persistence of communal perceptions and competition for the socio-economic resources are considered some of the reasons for the generation of communal ideologies and their transformation into major riots.

Identity schemes based on religion have become a major source of conflict not only in the international context but since the early 1990s it has also become a challenge for Indian democracy and secularism. The rise of majoritarian assertiveness is considered to have become institutionalized after the BJP that along with its *Hindutva* constituents gave political cohesiveness to a consolidating Hindu consciousness, formed a government in May 2014 with clear majority in general election. However, like all identity schemes the forging of a religious community glosses over internal differences within a particular religion to generate the 'we are all of the same kind' emotion.

Thus, differences of caste groups within a homogenous Hindu identity, linguistic and sectional differences within Islam are shelved to create a homogenous unified religious identity. In post-independence India, the majoritarian assertion has generated its own antithesis in the form of minority religions assertiveness and a resulting confrontational politics that undermines the syncretistic dimensions of the civil society in India.

The process through which this religious assertiveness is being increasingly institutionalized by a 'methodical rewriting of history' has the potential to reformulate India's national identity along communal trajectories. Have religion-based identity politics influenced by census and other related data sources is the question to be answered.

III

About the Volume

Chapters in this book discuss anxiety, myths and realities of religious demography as the subject is becoming more political in our times. The most prominent anxiety about Hindus being outnumbered continued in independent India. Such anxiety is expressed more in view of the nature of electoral politics in the country. In post-independence India, the majoritarian assertion has generated its own antithesis in the form of minority religious assertiveness and a resulting confrontational politics that undermines the syncretistic dimensions of the civil society in India. All the chapters written in this volume, written by experts in the field, dwell on the new and emerging trends in religious demography in the larger context of changes in India.

Leela Visaria addresses the myths prevalent in the country that persistent differentials in population growth are due to certain practices resulting in variations in fertility levels between various groups. The myth that this will upset the share of communities in India's demographic scenario needs to be addressed with careful analysis of available evidence. She analyses the available literature and examines the data in the context of socio-economic characteristics and geographic location of the religious communities in Indian states to show that these are far more important in influencing the fertility behaviour rather than religions *per se*. Both the onset and pace of fertility decline among various religious groups are examined to show the reality of fertility and to dispel the myth that demographic transition is confined to certain communities. In fact, careful analysis of demographic data in the chapter shows that there is sufficient evidence of convergence in the levels of fertility among the communities.

R.B. Bhagat throws light on Hindu and Muslim population growth rate. One of the first reactions arose at the beginning of the twentieth century when the 1901 census revealed a decline in the growth rate of Hindu population. This led to the articulation of a demographic theory of Hindus as a dying race. The fear of Hindus being outnumbered has since then erupted after almost every census. Concerns have been raised that a higher fertility among Muslims is essentially rooted in Islam and that Muslim men can have four wives. It has been clarified that Islam is not against family planning and that polygamy is not necessarily related to high fertility. On the contrary, it is found that women in polygamous marriages have lower fertility. Furthermore, it is also not true that the prevalence of polygamous marriages is higher among Muslims compared to Hindus. Bhagat argues that in independent India, there has been an effort to suppress caste data by not collecting data on castes except scheduled castes (SCs) and scheduled tribes (STs). On the contrary, there was no interference to the British legacy on the census of religious groups. As such in each census just after the release of data on religion, there was a heightened concern on the religious demography of India. It is ironical that while on the one hand there is euphoria about demographic dividend, on the other hand there are passions flared up on the relative growth rates of different religious communities. Bhagat furthers his argument, based on several studies, by narrating India's demographic reality is far more regional than the religious differences *per se* producing it.

Religion-based identity politics has been on the increase in India for over a century now. This trend has continued even after attaining Independence from the British rule in 1947 despite the fact that the country is a secular and democratic republic as per its Constitution. Mehar Singh Gill (2006) in his chapter focuses on three questions: (i) why Indian politics has become more and more focused on religion-based identity, (ii) is this trend likely to continue or change to an alternate focus of politics and (iii) which seems to be the more likely alternative? Gill further states that Hindus, who constitute a large majority in the country, have been as keen, if not more, as other religious minorities, to pursue religion-based identity politics. It arises mainly from four reasons: (i) religion-based partition of the country in 1947 which left behind its own religion-specific unhappy memories, fears and perceptions; (ii) the anxiety of the ruling class to weaken or even remove altogether the ethnic, regional, linguistic and cultural differences which, somehow, it perceives as obstacles for the unity of the country; (iii) to ensure that the political power stays in the hands of those whose main agenda is to bring about a homogenized sociopolitical space and (iv) it is much easier to build vote banks by appealing to religious sentiments than to socio-economic development programmes.

V. Sebastian explains that there are very few things in the post-Independent India which have gained permanence as much as religion as the marker of identity. However, it is not often remembered that the very taxonomy of 'religion' in India is a colonial invention, which had been reinforced time and again through the decennial census. Though belonging to the category of what historian Eric Hobsbawm has termed as the 'invented tradition', the taxonomy of 'religion' has gained the status, both as an objective reality and as an identity marker over the years. Most social scientists, the media and the 'religious' fundamentalists, tend to take the taxonomy of religion as a 'given' fact. This chapter looks at the dynamics which made 'religion' a central category in the identity politics in India and the role played by the decennial census in it.

Ambrose Pinto points out there are no major issues when one examines the quantitative aspects of demography such as composition, density, distribution, growth, movement, size and structure of the population. It is the qualitative aspects such as caste, religion, growth of communities, education quality, crime, development, diet and nutrition, social class, wealth and well-being that are made use of by communalists to further their ends. The increase or decrease of population of minority communities is interpreted by the communalists to suit their long-term interests. Pinto explains that population growth rates, when disaggregated along religious lines, provide fodder for religious extremists, who use the figures to fan communalism. Pinto refers Howard Wiggins and James Guyot who have noted that demographic changes can cause competing ethnic elites to worry that their groups' reduced numbers would cost them political clout and thereby 'precipitate ethnic group conflict'.

India is a vast complex country, with varied languages, cultures and religions. Even the words 'majority' and 'minority' lose their edge in India. There are 180 million Indian Muslims constituting the second largest Muslim bloc in the world. J.S. Bandukwala argues that a democracy operates on numbers. Census enumeration began in the late nineteenth century. The actual figures alarmed both Hindu and Muslim leaders at that time. Muslims read the figures as a sign that they can never come to power within India. This alarmed the landed aristocracy, particularly in North India. The result was a demand for separate electorates, which gradually evolved into a separate nation. Hindu leadership was equally disturbed, as figures showed a decrease in Hindu population percentage, but an increase in Muslim figures. This led to the Hindu Mahasabha and the RSS. It would not be out of place to say that the census played a vital part in the division of the country along religious lines. Bandukwala points out that Hindus and Muslims population percentages maybe stabilizing in India, as the fall in Muslim fertility rate is greater than the Hindu fertility rate. Ultimately, the fertility is related to living standards, education and income levels, combined with a feeling of security. India needs a communally free society, dedicated to growth and prosperity.

U.V. Somayajulu attempts to understand the demographic profile of Parsi population in India in terms of growth, marriages, fertility and migration. As per census 2011, there are about 69,000 Parsis. The number of Parsis declined in each decade since 1941. As per the National Commission for Minorities, there are many reasons for such steady decline in the population of Parsi community in India. One fifth of decrease in Parsi population is attributed to migration. Slower birth rate than death rate accounts for the rest. Demographic projections indicate that by 2020, the Parsi population would reach 23,000. Somayajulu points out that the Parsi community is the more westernized than other societies in India. They delay marriage while they save or wait for property. The Parsi couples began family planning decades ago to ensure that they pay for education of children, considered important for girls as well as boys. Parsi women are high achievers at work and they are reluctant to marry and start family at an early age, and being single is socially acceptable in the Parsi community. Somayajulu raises his concerns for the anxiety about disappearing population. More than one-third of Parsis marry non-Parsis. Parsi man's children will always be Parsi whoever he weds, but if Parsi woman marries outside the Parsi community, her sons and daughters are not deemed Parsis.

India is a multireligious society where almost 99 per cent of the total population falls into different major religious groups. Since religious identity, both social and political, plays a major part in Indian politics, politics manipulates these identities for its electoral success and thereby Indian politics, in a sense, is known as 'communal politics'. Himanshu Sekhar Mishra explains communal politics often result in communal riots which happen due to the manipulation of identity and demographic composition. Mishra argues that manipulation of demography and religious identity of local communities by the extreme forces are the main reasons for Kandhamal riots. Hindutva forces by using statistical formulations from the religious demography, aided the Hindu fear of alleged numerical decline which forced the demographic religious majority to project itself mentally as an endangered religious group. Such tendency has been linked up with Hindu national assertiveness and their communal perception since post-independence period which has produced its own antithesis in the form of minority religions assertiveness who foresee the possibility of losing autonomy of their religious and cultural life under such national assertiveness and communal perception. The chapter tries to investigate how the ethnic relation between *Kandhas* and *Panas* was converted into communal riot between Hindus and Christians in Kandhamal.

There can be no doubt that given the current debate on the topic, thorough probing is not only desirable but also very necessary. Crucial is the understanding of the dynamics of religious demography in the context of prevailing myths and realities. In all the chapters, an attempt has been made to understand and explain the myths and realities of religious demography with reference to various factors. This will aid in the decisive shaping of harmonious religious relations in India.

References

Basu, A.M. 1997. 'The Politicization of Fertility to Achieve Non-demographic Objectives', *Population Studies*, No. 51, pp. 5–18.

Bhagat, R.B. 2004. 'Fact and Fiction', *Economic and Political Weekly*, Vol. XXXIX, No. 39, September 25, pp. 4292–93.

Bhagat, R.B. 2013. 'Census Enumeration, Religious Identity and Communal Polarization in India', *Asian Ethnicity*, Vol. 14, No. 4, pp. 434–48.

Bhatia, P.S. 1990. 'Population Growth of Various Communities in India: Myth and Reality', *Demography India*, No. 19, pp. 121–9.

Brubaker, Rogers. 2004. 'Beyond Identity', *in Ethnicity without Groups*, Cambridge: Harvard University Press, pp. 28–63.

Census of India. 1931. Vol. XVII, Punjab, Part I: Report, 290.

Das, A.N. 1994. *India Invented: A Nation in the Making*, New Delhi: Manohar Publications.

Gupta, Charu. 2004. 'Censuses, Communalism, Gender and Identity: A Historical Perspective', *Economic and Political Weekly*, Vol. XXXIX, No. 39, September 25, pp. 4302–4.

http://indianexpress.com/article/opinion/columns/census-christians-conversions/(retrieved on February 16, 2017).

International Institute for Population Sciences and Macro International. India: National Family Health Survey (NFHS–2), 1998–1999; Mumbai: IIPS, 2000.

International Institute for Population Sciences and Macro International, India: National Family Health Survey (NFHS–3), 2005–2006; Mumbai: IIPS, 2007.

Jayaraj, D. and S. Subramanian. 2004. 'Manufacturing Hysteria on Census Inspired 'Nationalism'', *Economic and Political Weekly*, Vol. XXXIX, No. 39, September 25, pp. 4296–7.

Jones, K.W. 1981. 'Religious Identity and Indian Census', in *The Census in British India: New Perspectives*, N.G. Barrier (ed.), New Delhi: Manohar Publications, pp. 73–102.

Joshi, A.P., M.D. Srinivas and J.K. Bajaj. 2005. *Religious Demography of India*, Chennai: Centre for Policy Studies.

Kulkarni, P.M. 1996. *Differentials in the Population Growth of Hindus and Muslims in India, 1981–91*, Monograph Series No1, New Delhi: Population Foundation of India.

Mukherji, U.N. 1909. *Hindus: A Dying Race*, Calcutta: M. Bannerjee.

Murthy, Ponnapalli, Krishna and Faujdar, Ram. 2010. 'Religious Taxonomy of States and Districts in India: An Analysis Using a Standardized Index of Diversity (SID) of Religion', Working Paper 2, July 2010, IIPS – Mumbai.

Pew Research Center, 2015. 'The Future of World Religions: Population Growth Projections, 2010–2050', April 2.

Prakash, I. 1979. *They Count their Gains, We Calculate Our Losses*, New Delhi: Akhil Bharat Hindu Mahasabha.

Premi. M.K. 2004. 'Religion in India: A Demographic Perspective', *Economic and Political Weekly*, Vol. XXXIX, No. 39, pp. 4297–302.

Sengupta, C., A. Kumar and K.Y. Gandevia. 2003. *Communal Riots in Gujarat 2002: A Study of Contextual Factors* (unpublished manuscript). Mumbai: Tata Institute of Social Sciences.

Shraddhanand, S. 1926. *Hindu Sangathan: Saviour of the Dying Race*, Delhi: Arjun Press.

Raghuraman, Shankar. 2004. 'Muslims' Growth Rate much Lower', *The Times of India*, September 7, p. 1.

Visaria, Leela. 1974. 'Religious Differentials in Fertility', in *Population in India's Development*, 1947–2000, A. Bose et al. (ed.), Delhi: Vikash, pp. 361–74.

2 Demography of Religious Groups in India

Evidence versus Myths

Leela Visaria

The information on differential growth rates of Hindus and Muslims and the changes in their share in the total population of India ever since the question on religion was incorporated in the Indian censuses has stirred controversies.[1] The debates and discourse on religious demography have become intense in independent India after every decadal census count and has caused intense controversy more so in the last 25 years.[2] The recent availability of data from the 2011 census have shown that during the 2001–2011 decade, the share of Hindu population declined from 80.5 to 79.8 per cent; for the first time since India's independence its share went down below 80 per cent. The Registrar General and Census Commissioner who released the data on population (their number by sex separately for all the states) for the major religious communities from the 2011 census only towards the end of August 2015 has given rise to a wide speculation about the reasons for the delay of more than four years in the release of the data.[3] Also, the results have led to widespread coverage in the news media. Every major national and regional newspaper and television channel reported that the share of Hindus in India's population recorded 'sharpest dip' in a decade since independence and that the share of Muslims increased during 2001–2011 from 13.4 to 14.2 per cent. This has once again stirred the debate about the likely share of the two major religious groups of India in coming decades and possible explanations about the differential growth rates.

The increase in the number of analysts of population data, people trained in journalism, proliferation of media – both print and visual, slow but steady rise in religious fundamentalists and increase in the number of political leaders with communal divisive vote bank vision have all contributed to spread some information but a lot of misinformation about changing religious demography in India. Some researchers (demographers and also demagogues, whom Jeffery and Jeffery (2005) call 'saffron demographers') have contributed and raised passions among people by selectively using available information and doing simple extrapolations based on intercensal growth rates of Hindus and Muslims to argue that Hindus in India will become a minority in foreseeable future.[4] The information on the number or size, intercensal growth rate and changes in the share of the religious groups in the total population, especially on Hindu–Muslim differentials in population growth and its likely determinants, is often used and distorted by media because it makes a good story and headlines. Religious fundamentalists from both communities use the information to instigate people against each other. Even the political undercurrent and vote bank implications cannot be ignored or missed when the debates and discussion are charged with emotions.

In order to understand the basis on which hype and hysteria about religious demography are created, there is a need to examine the available population data and evidence dispassionately, objectively and analytically and with a historical perspective, rather than carrying out mechanistic and simplistic projections. This chapter presents the information compiled not only from various sources on numbers from the Indian censuses but also from other sources on underlying socio-economic and cultural factors besides religion affiliation that influence behaviour, attitudes and practices. The evidence on trends and changes in them in the recent past are likely to inform the observed differentials in population growth rates of Hindus and Muslims in India and the likely future paths of the two communities.

Size, Share and Growth Rates of Population of Religious Groups

A question on a person's (generally of the household head) religion has been asked in the Indian census since 1881. The categories have become more or less the same at least since 1961 and they are Hindus, Muslims, Christians, Sikhs, Buddhists, Jains and others.[5] Until 1931, the British census commissioners tabulated and provided information on age distribution of the major religious groups. After independence, given the sensitivity about religion, only information available in the public domain until 1991 was the number of people counted in each religious group. The data have been available up to district level.[6] From the available information, it is possible to calculate intercensal growth rates of religious group and their percentage share in the population. Since the changes in the trends in these parameters has acquired political significance, as noted above, it is important to document them.

After growing at close to 2.5 per cent annually between 1961 and 1981, India's population growth has slowed down; during 2001–2011, it grew at 1.77 per cent per annum that is the slowest growth experienced and has been hailed by many that India's efforts at lowering fertility are paying dividends. Tables 2.1–2.3 show the population of India by major religious groups since 1961, their share in the total population and the inter-decadal growth rate of each group. These tables highlight the fact that the four major religious groups – Hindus, Muslims, Christians and Sikhs – have constituted 98 to 98.5 per cent of India's population throughout the 50-year period between 1961 and 2011. The 'other' category includes people belonging to numerically very small religious groups such as Zoroastrianism or Judaism and those who have chosen not to state their religion. While the number of Parsis and Jews has steadily declined over time, those who have reported that they do not practice any religion has steadily increased since 1961 but much more so between 1991 and 2011 than during the earlier enumerations; their number doubled from 1.5 to 3.1 million in three decades between 1961 and 1991 and increased to 7.9 million or by 2.5 times in 20 years between 1991 and 2011. Similarly, the number of people who reported that they profess 'no religion', although small in size around 0.1 million until 1981 increased to 2.9 million by 2011. Very likely, majority of such respondents live in metropolitan cities and have education beyond high school, who have consciously reported that they do not profess any structured religion in which belief systems and rituals are systematically arranged and formally established.

Table 2.1 *Population of India by Religious Groups, 1961–2011 (figures in million)*

Religious Groups/Year	*1961*	*1971*	*1981*	*1991*	*2001*	*2011*
All Religions	439.23	547.95	665.29	838.58	1,028.61	1,210.85
Hindus	366.53	453.29	549.78	687.65	827.58	966.26
Muslims	46.94	61.42	75.51	101.60	138.19	172.25
Christians	10.73	14.22	16.17	19.64	24.08	27.82
Sikhs	7.85	10.38	13.08	16.26	19.22	20.83
Buddhists	3.26	3.81	4.72	6.39	7.96	8.44
Jains	2.03	2.60	3.21	3.35	4.23	4.45
Others	1.50	2.18	2.77	3.07	6.64	7.94
Religion not stated	0.11	0.04	0.06	0.42	0.73	2.87

Table 2.2 shows the share of all the religious groups in the total population since 1961. The slow but steady declining share of Hindus and increasing share of Muslims has aroused communal passions. The share of Hindus slowly but steadily declined from 84.4 per cent in the total population of India to 79.8 per cent in 2011 and that of Muslims increased from 9.9 to 14.2 per cent in the same period. The share of the other groups has more or less

remained the same over time, although as shown in Table 2.3, their growth rates have fluctuated to some extent. Together the other four religious groups – Christians, Sikhs, Buddhists and Jains – constituted only 5 per cent of the total population in 2011, but their influence on India's economy and on other sectors has been noteworthy.

Table 2.2 *Per cent Share of Religious Groups in the Total Population, India, 1961–2011 (adjusted)*

Religious Groups/Year	*1961*	*1971*	*1981*	*1991*	*2001*	*2011*
All Religions	100.0	100.0	100.0	100.0	100.0	100.0
Hindus	84.4	83.5	83.1	82.4	81.4	79.8
Muslims	9.9	10.4	10.9	11.7	12.4	14.2
Christians	2.4	2.6	2.5	2.3	2.3	2.3
Sikhs	1.8	1.9	2.0	2.0	1.9	1.7
Buddhists	0.7	0.7	0.7	0.8	0.8	0.7
Jains	0.5	0.5	0.5	0.4	0.4	0.4
Others	0.3	0.4	0.4	0.4	0.7	0.7
Religion not stated	Neg.	Neg.	Neg.	Neg.	Neg.	0.2

Proportionate share is calculated after excluding Jammu and Kashmir and Assam for all decades from 1961 to 2001. No census was conducted in Assam in 1981 and in Jammu and Kashmir in 1991.

Neg. means negligible.

Within India, the rate of population growth has varied a great deal over time among the small religious communities. The Christian population grew at a faster rate than all the other groups during 1961–1971; their faster growth rate is attributed partly to conversion, especially from among the SC and ST population, to Christianity. However, their decadal growth rate during 2001–2011 was 15.5 per cent, or lower than the all India growth rate. Compared to the earlier decades when Sikhs experienced relatively high growth, since 1991 it has slowed down significantly; in fact during 2001–2011 there was only a little over 8 per cent increase in their population. The 1981–1891 decadal growth rate of 36 per cent among Buddhists is also partly attributed to conversion as neo-Buddhists by SC population mainly in the western state of Maharashtra. But since then, all the numerically small religious groups have recorded low growth rate in recent decades. Some of the fluctuations, especially among the Jains as well as among other small religious groups, can partly be explained by the blurring of boundaries between the groups, and reporting, enumerating or recording religion is not always perceived as important.

However, what has received attention of most is that throughout the period 1961–2011 Muslim population growth rate has been higher than that of the Hindu population. Between 1961 and 1991, Hindus grew at an average annual rate ranging between 2.3 and 2.4 per cent, whereas Muslim population recorded annual growth rate between 3.1 and 3.3 per cent during this period. Since then the growth rate has slowed down for both the communities as shown in Table 2.3. The 2011–2011 decadal growth of Hindu population was 16.8 per cent and that of Muslim population was 24.6 per cent. Even though the pace of decline of population growth rate of Muslims has become faster since 1991, the projections and predictions, solely based on the numbers, continue to be made and statements such as that the Muslim growth rate is almost 1.5 times higher than the rate of Hindu population growth catch attention of lay people. Similarly, projection about when Muslims will overtake Hindus continue to be made that arouse passions of zealots. Even Sachar Committee's report, taking into account the falling growth rate of Muslims during 1991–2001 estimated that by 2100 the Muslim population will stabilize between 17 and 21 per cent of India's total population, received more attention than some of its other important findings dealing with socio-economic characteristics of Muslims. This may be a far cry from some of the doomsday scenarios that some forecast but they do contribute to the communal passions and fail to take into account the likely and inevitable changes that all population groups would experience in the coming years that would influence their demographic parameters.

Table 2.3 *Growth Rate of Religious Groups, 1961–2011*

Religious Groups/Period	*1961–1971*	*1971–1981*	*1981–1991*	*1991–2001*	*2001–2011*
All Religions	24.8	24.8	23.8	21.5	17.7
Hindus	23.4	24.2	22.8	20.0	16.8
Muslims	31.2	30.8	32.9	29.3	24.6
Christians	36.0	19.2	17.0	22.1	15.5
Sikhs	32.0	26.2	25.5	16.9	8.4
Buddhists	17.0	25.4	36.0	23.2	6.0
Jains	28.5	23.7	4.0	26.0	5.2
Others	97.7	26.6	13.2	111.3	19.6
Religion not stated	–65.7	67.1	573.5	76.3	293.1

In Table 2.4, data are presented for 11 states of India on the number and share of Hindu and Muslim population for three decadal years 1991, 2001 and 2011. The states are selected for their sizeable Muslim population; according to 2011 census, 150 out of 172 million or 87 per cent of all Muslims enumerated in India lived in the 11 states out of the total of 29 states and 7 union territories. Between 1991 and 2011, the share of Muslim population in all these 11 states has increased and conversely that of Hindus has declined in most of states in the 20-year period. Within these 11 states, Jammu and Kashmir with 68 per cent of its total population enumerated as Muslim in 2011 is predominantly a Muslim state. Kerala and West Bengal are the other two states that have more than a quarter of their population enumerated as Muslims. In the most populous state of India – Uttar Pradesh – although Muslims constitute 19 per cent of its total population, they represent 22 per cent of all Muslims (38.5 million) living in India. The share of Muslims in the total population of Assam increased from 28.4 per cent in 1991 to 34.2 per cent in 2011; the rapid increase was recorded in the districts bordering Bangladesh and is attributed to immigration that is believed to be largely illegal and undertaken to escape from poverty and unemployment in Bangladesh. The West Bengal districts bordering with Bangladesh also recorded high growth rate among Muslims.

Table 2.4 *Population of Hindus and Muslims in Selected States in 1991–2011 (in millions and percentages in parentheses)*

States	*1991*		*2001*		*2011*	
	Hindu	*Muslim*	*Hindu*	*Muslim*	*Hindu*	*Muslim*
Assam	15.1 (67.2)	6.4 (28.4)	17.3 (64.9)	8.2 (30.9)	19.2 (61.5)	10.7 (34.2)
Andhra P.	59.3 (89.1)	6.0 (8.9)	67.8 (89.0)	7.0 (9.2)	74.8 (88.5)	8.1 (9.6)
Bihar	71.2 (82.4)	12.8 (14.8)	69.1 (83.2)	13.7 (16.5)	86.1 (82.7)	17.6 (16.9)
Gujarat	36.0 (89.5)	3.6 (8.7)	45.1 (89.1)	4.6 (9.1)	53.5 (88.6)	5.9 (9.7)
Jammu and Kashmir	NA	NA	3.0 (29.6)	6.8 (67.0)	3.6 (28.4)	8.6 (68.3)
Karnataka	38.4 (85.4)	5.2 (11.6)	44.3 (83.9)	6.5 (12.2)	51.3 (84.0)	7.9 (12.9)
Kerala	16.7 (57.3)	6.8 (23.3)	17.9 (56.2)	7.9 (24.7)	18.3 (54.7)	8.9 (26.6)
Maharashtra	64.0 (81.1)	7.6 (9.7)	77.9 (80.4)	10.3 (10.6)	89.7 (79.8)	13.0 (11.5)
Rajasthan	39.2 (89.1)	3.5 (8.0)	50.2 (88.7)	4.8 (8.5)	60.7 (88.5)	6.2 (9.1)
Uttar Pradesh	113.7 (81.7)	24.1 (17.3)	134.0 (80.6)	30.7 (18.5)	159.3 (79.7)	38.5 (19.3)
West Bengal	50.9 (74.7)	17.0 (23.4)	58.1 (72.5)	20.2 (25.2)	64.4 (70.5)	24.7 (27.0)
Total of 11 states	504.5 (73.4)	93.0 (91.5)	584.7 (70.7)	121.7 (88.1)	680.9 (70.5)	150.1 (87.2)
Rest of States	183.2 (26.6)	8.6 (8.5)	242.7 (29.3)	16.5 (11.9)	346.1 (29.5)	22.0 (12.8)
Total Population	687.7 (82.4)	101.6 (11.7)	827.4 (81.4)	138.2 (12.4)	966.3 (79.8)	172.1 (14.2)

Note: Among the large states in terms of total population, Madhya Pradesh and Tamil Nadu are not included because the share of Muslim population in these two states in 2011 was around 6 per cent and their absolute number was 4.8 million in Madhya Pradesh and 4.2 million in Tamil Nadu. They are included in the rest of states.

Explanations for Differential Rates of Population Growth

The higher growth rate of Muslims compared to that Hindus has been attributed to their higher fertility and lower use of contraceptives to limit fertility. Several hypotheses have been advanced to explain fertility differences between religious groups that range from theology or religiosity, socio-economic factors, minority status, interaction, differential access to services and so on (Alagrajan and Kulkarni 2005; Iyer 2002a; McQuillan 2004). It is argued that the precepts or teachings of Islam influence fertility behaviour and ordinary Muslims accept and follow the teachings unquestioningly irrespective of their socio-economic or demographic characteristics. It is also hypothesized that since Muslims are a minority group in India, in order to overcome political and social insecurity, they have higher fertility with a view to increase their share in the population. The more widely prevalent hypothesis is that socio-economic factors influence fertility behaviour and on most counts Indian Muslims are worse off compared to the other religious groups. It is also postulated that Muslims have less access to health and family planning services that results in high fertility among them.

Since the unit level data from the three National Family and Health Surveys conducted during 1992–1993, 1998–1999 and 2005–2006 have become available to all, several studies and analyses have been carried out by researchers to explain the fertility differentials between Hindus and Muslims (Alagrajan and Kulkarni 2005; Bhat 1996; Bhat and Zavier 2005; Dharmalingam and Morgan 2004; Dharmalingam, Navaneetham and Morgan 2005; James and Nair 2005; Mishra 2004; Rajan 2005). In fact, during 2005, *Economic and Political Weekly*, (See *EPW*'s Vol. 40, No. 5, January 20, 2005) commissioned a series of papers to examine religion and fertility behaviour in India. Most of the analyses undertaken by demographers in that volume were based on the available National Family Health Survey (NFHS) conducted during 1992–1993 and

1998–1999 and the data from the Censuses of India, especially the 2001 census.

Fertility Levels

The available data permitted the authors to estimate the fertility levels of all major religious groups but they primarily focused on Hindu–Muslim fertility levels for obvious reasons. They noted that the level of fertility among Muslims has been higher than that among Hindus not only in the country as a whole but also in all the major states. Over time, as shown in Figure 2.1, the TFR of Muslims since 1984, when such data became available for India from the special sample registration survey conducted by the Census Commissioner, the differentials have persisted. Albeit, the differences in TFR between all religious groups have narrowed in 2005–2006 compared to the earlier periods, indicating a trend towards what some demographers have termed as 'convergence' (Dharmalingam et. al. 2005; Kulkarni and Alagrajan 2005). As Table 2.5 and Figure 2.1 show, the pace of decline in Muslim fertility has been faster than that of the Hindu fertility in the recent years. Fertility among Muslims started declining at a later time period compared to the other religious groups but the pace of decline has picked up. The decline in Muslim TFR in just over a decade or in about 13 years between 1992–1993 and 2005–2006 was almost 30 per cent compared to 18 per cent among Hindus during the same period. The late entrants to demographic transition are generally found to experience faster decline for several reasons. World over this has been the case. Indian Muslims are no exception to this. The argument of 'pervasiveness of Hindu–Muslim differences in fertility behaviour', propagated by some research analysts (Reddy 2003), often based on single point data or current level, and also by Hindu right-wing scholars does not hold true when rates or pace of change over time are examined.

Table 2.5 *Total Fertility Rates (TFRs) among Hindus, Muslims and Other Religious Groups in India (various sources and years)*

TFR	*Hindu*	*Muslim*	*Christian*	*Sikh*	*Others*	*All*
SRS 1984	4.5	5.6	3.8	3.7	4.4	4.5
NFHS 1992–1993	3.3	4.4	2.9	2.4	2.8	3.4
NFHS 1998–1999	2.8	3.6	2.4	2.3	2.3	2.9
NFHS 2005–2006	2.7	3.1 3.1	2.4	2.0	2.7	2.7
% decline between 1984 and 1992–1993	21.4	21.4	23.7	35.1	26.4	24.4
% decline between 1992–1993 and 2005–2006	18.2	29.5	17.2	16.7	3.6	20.6

Figure 2.1 *Total Fertility Rates among Four Major Religious Groups, India, 1984–2005–2006*

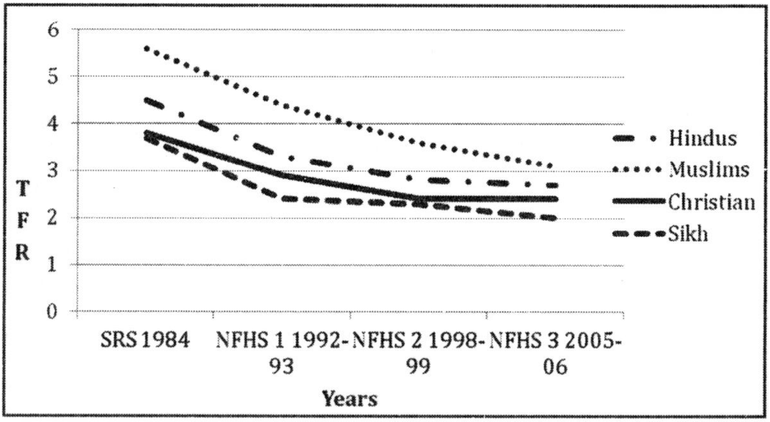

Source: SRS 1984; NFHS 1, 2, 3: 1992–93; 1998–99; 2005–6.

It is equally important to examine both the level and the pace of decline in fertility (TFR) among Hindus and Muslims over the three NFHS in the major states of India. As Table 2.6 shows, by 2005–2006 the Muslim TFR had reached below 2.5 children per woman in several states such as Andhra Pradesh, Jammu and Kashmir, Karnataka and Kerala. In Gujarat and Maharashtra, Muslim TFR was below 3. There is no denying of the fact that fertility transition is clearly under way even among Muslims in several states of India. Further, in the states where Muslims form at least 10 per cent of the total population, the rate of decline in fertility of Muslims between 1992–1993 and 2005–2006 has been higher than that among the Hindus with the exception of Uttar Pradesh and Assam and to a small extent Gujarat. Assam state is a special case in flex and turmoil with a large border with Bangladesh and immigration of poor Muslims to the state. The pace of fertility decline in economically underdeveloped states of Bihar and Uttar Pradesh has been slow for both Hindus and Muslims, which many attribute to the low socio-economic indicators of individuals and to the underdevelopment indicators and poor infrastructure of the region. The TFR of Hindus in Bihar and Uttar Pradesh estimated by NFHS–3 for 2005–2006 at 3.9 and 3.7, respectively, are the highest in India and so is the case with that of Muslim TFR of 4.8 and 4.3, respectively.

Table 2.6 *Total Fertility of Hindus and Muslims in Selected States of India, NFHS–1 to NFHS–3*

TFR	*NFHS–1 (1992–1993)*		*NFHS–2 (1998–1999)*		*NFHS–3 (2005–2006)*		*% decline between 1992–1993 and 2005–2006*	
	Hindu	*Muslim*	*Hindu*	*Muslim*	*Hindu*	*Muslim*	*Hindu*	*Muslim*
Assam	2.9	5.0	2.0	3.1	2.0	3.6	31.0	28.0
Andhra Pradesh	2.6	2.9	2.2	2.5	1.8	1.9	30.8	34.5
Bihar	3.8	5.2	3.4	4.4	3.9	4.8	-2.6	7.7
Gujarat	3.0	3.3	2.7	3.2	2.4	2.7	20.0	18.2
Jammu and Kashmir	3.0	3.9	2.7	2.7	2.2	2.5	36.4	56.0
Karnataka	2.7	3.9	2.0	2.8	2.1	2.2	22.2	43.6
Kerala	1.7	3.0	1.7	2.5	1.6	2.5	5.9	16.7
Maharashtra	2.7	4.1	2.5	3.3	2.0	2.9	25.9	29.3
Rajasthan*	3.7	4.0	3.7	4.9	3.2	4.0	15.6	0.0
Uttar Pradesh	4.8	5.3	3.9	4.8	3.7	4.3	22.9	18.9
West Bengal	2.5	4.6	2.0	3.3	1.9	3.2	24.0	30.4

* Some concerns were reported with the quality of fieldwork carried out in Rajasthan during the first NFHS and thereby some of the data were subject of scrutiny. The fertility rates of Muslims across three surveys do not show any consistent pattern that is evident in all the other states.

Since TFR is a period indicator that measures the average number of children a woman would have over her reproductive lifetime if she experiences the given age-specific fertility schedule at the time of data collection. We therefore examine the three NFHS data on completed family size measured as the mean number of children ever born to women aged 40–49, who would most unlikely to bear any more children. This measure, termed as 'cohort measure of fertility', refers to the fertility experience of a cohort of women born 40–49 years ago. Table 2.7 shows the average number of children born to women aged 40–49 of major religious groups according tc the three NFHS. It shows that the average number of children born to Christian and Sikh women has been lower than the average for the country as a whole and has been higher among Muslim women throughout the three surveys. But note that the per cent decline among Muslims is greater over the 13-year period compared to that for all the other groups. However, the quantum of decline is not as high as has been with that in TFR. What this implies is that the fertility has begun to decline among Muslims later with a time lag of about a decade compared to the other religious groups.

Table 2.7 *Average Number of Children Born to Women Aged 40–49 in NFHS–1 to NFHS–3*

Religion	*NFHS–1 (1992–1993)*	*NFHS–2 (1998–1999)*	*NFHS–3 (2005–2006)*	*% decline between 1992–1993 and 2005–2006*
Hindu	4.78	4.34	3.97	16.9
Muslim	5.83	5.72	4.60	21.1
Christian	4.01	3.47	3.27	18.5
Sikh	3.99	3.59	3.56	10.8
All	4.84	4.45	4.00	17.4

Data available from NFHS–2 and NFHS–3 for the major states on the mean number of children born to Hindu and Muslim women aged 40–49 or completed fertility of this cohort of women are shown in Table 2.8. Similar data are not available from the first NFHS conducted during 1992–1993 for the states. The data show the cumulated experienced of women born roughly during 1950 and 1965 and who reached the beginning of their reproductive span during 1965–1980 or at a time when the national family planning programme was barely picking up.[7] The number of children born to Muslim women aged 40–49 has been higher than to Hindu women according to both the surveys in all the states. What is worth noting is that the onset of fertility decline among Muslims began later but has picked up momentum in recent years. Even in the span of about 7 years between the NFHS conducted in 1998–1999 and 2005–2006, the cumulated cohort fertility of Muslim women declined in several states, especially those in southern and western India by about one child. Andhra Pradesh recorded a decline from 5.8 to 4.1 children for the two cohorts that reached ages 40–49 in 1998–1999 and 2005–2006, respectively. The decline among Muslims in Karnataka was also of a similar magnitude. Except for a few core North India states such as Bihar and Uttar Pradesh, fertility transition among Muslims is clearly underway and the reversal of this trend is most unlikely.[8]

Table 2.8 *Average Number of Children Born to Hindu and Muslim Women Aged 40–49 for Major States of India, NFHS–2 and NFHS–3*

States	*NFHS–2 (1998–1999)*		*NFHS–3 (2005–2006)*		*% Decline between 1998–1999 and 2005–2006*	
	Hindu	*Muslim*	*Hindu*	*Muslim*	*Hindu*	*Muslim*
Assam	4.0	5.3	3.5	5.4	14.3	–0.2
Andhra Pradesh	3.9	5.8	3.3	4.1	20.5	41.5
Bihar	5.0	6.4	5.1	6.4	28.0	0.0
Gujarat	4.0	4.7	3.5	3.7	14.3	27.0
Jammu and Kashmir	4.7	4.9	3.4	4.4	38.2	11.4
Karnataka	4.0	5.8	3.1	4.3	29.0	34.9
Kerala	2.6	4.3	2.2	3.5	18.2	22.9
Maharashtra	3.7	4.6	3.3	4.4	15.6	4.5
Rajasthan	5.3	6.5	4.9	5.5	8.2	18.2
Uttar Pradesh	5.6	6.8	5.5	6.3	1.8	7.9
West Bengal	5.3	6.0	3.1	5.2	19.3	18.2

Contraceptive Use Explaining Fertility Differentials

Among the major proximate determinants of fertility identified by Bongaarts (1978), namely, marriage, contraceptive use, postpartum amenorrhea or infecundability and abortion, the differences in contraceptive use among Hindus and Muslims in all the states of India were established as the most important factor explaining fertility differentials (James and Nair 2005). The decomposition exercise was carried out using one point survey data from the NFHS–2 of 1998–1999 rather than examining changes in the contribution of the four proximate determinants over time. However, by comparing their effect on total fecundity (meaning natural fertility and referring to the number of children born to a woman in the absence of any fertility inhibiting factors) in demographically advanced southern states and all India, the authors found that with the exception of Kerala, the use of contraception is the major factor among both Hindus and Muslims in suppressing total fecundity. However, what is important to note is that the Hindu–Muslim differences in contraceptive use in the southern states are narrower compared to the other states implying that fertility transition and steady increase in contraception to regulate fertility are well underway.

Table 2.9 for all India and Table 2.10 for the eleven states with sizeable Muslim population convincingly show that contraceptive use among Muslims has rapidly increased since the 1990s. In fact, between 1992–1993 and 2005–2006, the contraceptive use among Muslims in the country as a whole increased from 28 to 46 per cent or an increase of 65 per cent in the 13-year period. During the same period, the Hindus contraceptive use increased from 42 to 58 per cent or by 39 per cent. Clearly, Muslims have longer ground to cover having started from a relatively low level and late in time but they are catching up at a faster rate regarding the use of contraception.

Table 2.9 *Contraceptive Prevalence Rate among Currently Married Hindus and Muslim Women Aged 15–49 in India, NFHS–1 to NFHS–3*

Religion/NFHS	*Hindu*	*Muslim*	*All Religions*
NFHS–1 1992–1993	41.6	27.7	40.7
NFHS–2 1998–1999	49.2	37.0	48.2
NFHS–3 2005–2006	57.8	45.7	56.3
% Increase between 1992–1993 and 2005–2006	38.9	65.0	38.3

Table 2.10 *Contraceptive Prevalence Rate (CPR) among Hindus and Muslims in Major States of India, NFHS–2 and NFHS–3*

States	*NFHS–2 (1998–1999)*		*NFHS–3 (2005–2006)*		*% increase in CPR between 1998–1999 and 2005–2006*	
	Hindu	*Muslim*	*Hindu*	*Muslim*	*Hindu*	*Muslim*
All India	49.2	37.0	57.8	45.7	17.5	23.5
Assam	48.6	33.5	61.3	46.1	26.1	37.6
Andhra Pradesh	61.1	46.7	68.1	62.3	11.4	33.4
Bihar	27.3	9.1	36.9	19.0	35.2	108.8
Gujarat	59.0	58.0	67.0	60.9	13.6	5.0
Jammu and Kashmir	52.6	46.1	56.5	49.1	7.4	6.5
Karnataka	60.1	44.2	64.7	56.2	7.7	27.1
Kerala	71.6	47.2	74.4	54.8	3.9	16.1
Maharashtra	62.0	49.1	68.0	58.3	9.7	18.7
Rajasthan	41.4	25.4	47.8	38.8	15.5	52.8
Uttar Pradesh	29.2	21.0	46.3	29.6	58.6	41.0
West Bengal	69.8	56.3	75.1	61.1	7.6	8.5

This is amply demonstrated in Table 2.10. In several better-developed states (Andhra Pradesh, Gujarat, Jammu and Kashmir, Karnataka, Kerala, Maharashtra and West Bengal), contraceptive use rate among Muslims was higher than their all-India contraceptive use rate of 46 per cent in 2005–2006. According to 2011 census, 45 per cent of all Muslims resided in these seven states. In fact, with the exception of Jammu and Kashmir with contraceptive use of 49 per cent, in the other six states it had already reached above 55 per cent. Further, Table 2.10 shows that in a short span of seven years, contraceptive use rate among Muslims increased at a faster rate in almost all the states compared to that among the Hindus and the difference between the two religious groups has narrowed. As shown earlier in Table 2.6, the Muslim TFR in these states had reached below 3 in 2005–2006. There is no reason to believe that the fertility transition that has set in nearly half of the Muslim population in India will falter or abate in the coming years.

On the other hand, although the contraceptive use rate among Muslims in Bihar is more than doubled between 1998–1999 and 2005–2006 from 9 to 19 per cent and increased by 41 per cent in Uttar Pradesh from 21 to 30 per cent, these two states with nearly a third of India's Muslim population have a long way to catch up with those living elsewhere in India. Evidently, the onset of fertility decline and increase in contraceptive use has begun a few years later for both Hindus and Muslims in these two states as well as in Rajasthan but it is quite likely that the pace of decline in fertility and increase in contraception would be faster and with some time lag, they will catch up with those in the rest of the country. The process of fertility transition seems to have set in and is very unlikely to stop or even slow down.

Figure 2.2 ***Contraceptive Use by Method among Hindus and Muslims, 1992–1993 and 2005–2006***

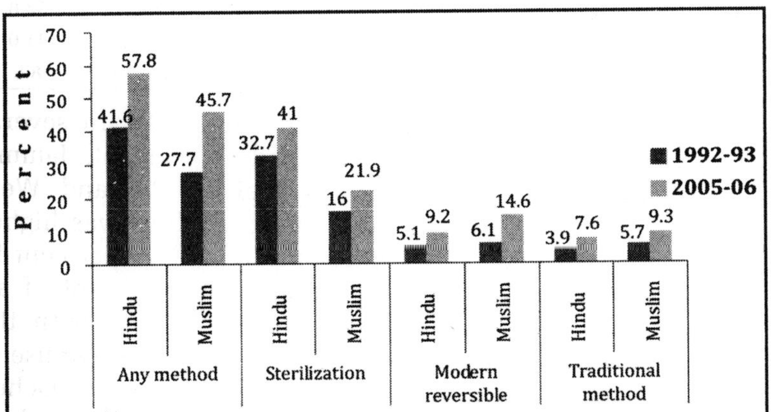

Source: NFHS 1, 3: 1992–93; 2005–06.

The support for the assertion made above comes from three interrelated pieces of evidence. One, the increase in all the contraceptive methods between 1992–1993 and 2005–2006 is quite evident not only among Hindus but also significantly so among Muslims as shown in Figure 2.2. While the use of sterilization among Muslims was low compared to that among Hindus, contrary to popular perception in 2005–2006 nearly one in four contracepting Muslim couples chose sterilization as a method to limit their family size. Also, compared to Hindus, both modern reversible methods and traditional methods are more popular among Muslim couples. Contraceptive prevalence rate increases at a faster rate when couples rely on reversible methods. Sterilization as a method is generally resorted to when couples have completed their family size and also take into account not only the past but also possible future loss of a child due to mortality.

Two, while accepting the fact that women respond to the question on the desire to limit fertility taking into account the number of children they have already given birth to, the per cent of women desiring to limit fertility after two children as shown in Figure 2.3 has gone up among Muslim women from 39 in 1992–1993 to close to 75 per cent in 2005–2006. In a span of 13 years, the per cent of Muslim women desiring to limit children to two has nearly doubled signifying a steep attitudinal change. The increase in the proportion of Hindu women desiring to limit fertility after two children increased from 61 to 84 per cent between 1992–1993 and 2005–2006. Evidently, the difference between the two communities in desire to limit childbearing to just two children has also narrowed in recent years. Women with three children desiring not to have any additional children increased from 78 to 91 per cent among Hindu women but from 60 to 85 per cent among Muslim women between 1992–1993 and 2005–2006. In the short span of 13 years, difference in the desire for additional children between Hindu and a Muslim woman with three children has virtually disappeared.

Figure 2.3 *Desire to Limit Childbearing by Number of Living Children among Hindus and Muslims, NFHS–1, NFHS–2 and NFHS–3*

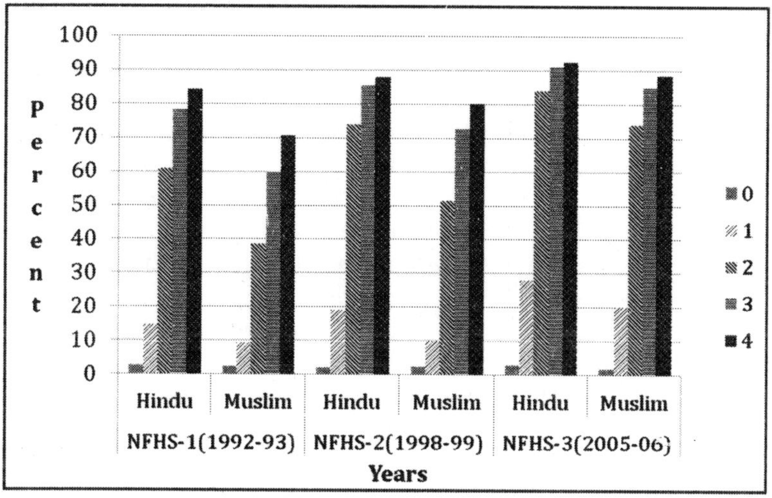

Source: NFHS 1, 2, 3: 1992-93; 1998–99; 2005–06.

The third piece of evidence that Muslim women do want to control their fertility comes from the percentage reporting unmet need for family planning. As shown in Figure 2.4 compared to Hindus and also other religious groups (data for the numerically small religious groups not shown), Muslim women reported higher level of unmet need for both spacing and limiting methods. The assertion often made that Muslims are averse to using any method of contraceptives including the methods to limit family planning does not hold true. The reality born by the evidence from the national level surveys is that fertility of Muslims has started falling, desire for many children is weakening, contraceptive use of all methods of family planning is increasing and the need for family planning is growing. This is true in all the states of India. Although a short time lag may be just of a decade in the onset of these crucial indicators of fertility transition within the Muslim population, the change is not only perceptible but also documented with available data.

Figure 2.4 *Unmet Need for Family Planning among Hindus and Muslims, NFHS–1, NFHS–2 and NFHS–3*

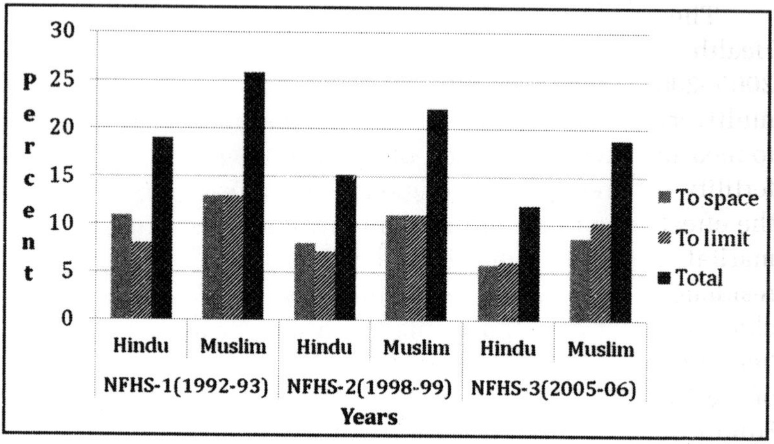

Source: Same as Figure 2.3.

Socio-economic Factors Explaining Fertility Differentials

While most of the analyses undertaken by population scientists have attributed the decline in fertility and the differentials to variations in the socio-economic characteristics of the two religious groups, when crude birth rates and TFRs for Hindus and Muslims were estimated at district level from the 2001 census data, Rajan (2005) noted that there is a regional variation in fertility in India. Fertility has been higher in the northern region compared to the southern and western districts of India, irrespective of religion affiliation. A similar exercise, carried out by Bose (2005) using the 2001 census data from 49 predominately Muslim districts, also noted that the geographical location and economic conditions rather than religion influence people's behaviour including that with regard to fertility. These analyses reconfirm that there is a regional variation in fertility in India estimated on the basis of 1891–1931 censuses of Indian subcontinent (including Pakistan and Bangladesh) in addition to the religion professed by people (Visaria and Visaria 1982). Within a region, higher fertility among Muslims compared to Hindus was found to exist, but the regional factor influencing behaviour of all cannot be undermined or ignored.

The data available from the three National Family Health Surveys conducted in the decade of 1990s and in 2005–2006 have enabled demographers to carry out multivariate analysis and use multi-level regression models to measure the contribution of socio-economic factors to the fertility differentials by religion. Even after controlling for the effects of a range of demographic variables (such as age, marital duration), household level factors (such as caste, residence, household's economic status), socio-economic characteristics of respondents (such as woman's education, her and her husband's occupation, exposure to media, index of woman's autonomy), the analyses showed that Hindu-Muslim differences in fertility could not primarily be attributed to differences in socio-economic factors. There was a net or residual effect of religion on fertility after statistically controlling for the effect of socio-economic factors (Alagrajan and Kulkarni 2005; Bhat and Zavier 2005; Dharmalingam et al. 2005).

However, it is important to closely examine the fact that a larger proportion of Muslims compared to Hindus (when SC and ST groups are excluded, almost all of them are enumerated as Hindu) are less educated and poorer since among the range of socio-economic factors education has been shown to the most important determinant of fertility behaviour. It is therefore useful to look at the increase in education among Hindus and Muslims between 2001 and 2011 – both in terms of literacy rates and by the level of education, especially at secondary level and beyond since the education impact on fertility is expected to be stronger at higher level of education.[9] Table 2.11 shows the literacy rates that have been calculated for population six years and above for the major religious groups. The two important facts that emerge from the table are that there has been an improvement in attainment of literacy among both males and females of all the religious groups but the increase among females has been higher than among males signifying that the gender gap is narrowing across religion.[10] Equally important is that the improvement in literacy rate is greater among Muslim males and females compared to that among Hindus, signifying that the gap in literacy levels between these two religious groups is also narrowing.

Table 2.11 *Literacy Rate in 6+ Population by Sex and Religion, 2001 and 2011*

Religion	*Per cent Literate*		*Per cent Literate*		*Per cent Literate*	
	2001 Males	*2011 Males*	*2001 Females*	*2011 Females*	*2001 All*	*2011 All*
Hindu	76.2	81.7	53.2	64.3	65.1	73.3
Muslim	67.6	74.7	50.1	62.0	59.1	68.5
Christian	84.4	87.7	76.2	81.4	80.3	85.4
Sikh	75.2	80.0	63.1	70.2	69.4	75.4
All religions	75.3	80.9	53.7	64.6	64.8	73.0

Further, data from 2001 and 2011 censuses on the level of education are presented in Table 2.12 for Muslims and Hindus. It has been shown that higher the level of women's education attainment, the fewer children she is likely to bear. Thus, there is a negative correlation between the level of education and TFR. An increase in the level of education of girls works in many ways. It contributes to delaying girls' marriage. It has also been argued that when women receive higher education, their exposure to different ideas and knowledge about prenatal and child health care increases. Also, they gain greater confidence that their children will survive beyond infancy and early childhood and are able and willing to access family planning services to limit the number of children they desire and have and to whom they can provide education and other facilities.

With this well-established relation between level of education and fertility in focus, we examined the available data to discern the increase in attainment of education beyond primary level among women and men of the two major religious communities. Despite the fact that

Table 2.12 *Per cent of Hindus and Muslims by Sex by Levels of Education, 2001 and 2011*

Education Level	*Hindu Males*		*Muslim Males*		*All Religion Males*	
	2001	*2011*	*2001*	*2011*	*2001*	*2011*
Secondary level/matric	9.9	10.7	6.6	7.3	9.6	10.2
Higher secondary	4.9	7.8	2.8	5.0	4.6	7.5
Technical or non-technical diploma or degree	0.6	1.0	0.3	0.6	0.6	1.0
Graduate and above	5.1	7.3	2.4	3.5	4.8	6.8
% with education secondary level and above	20.5	26.8	12.1	16.4	19.6	25.5
	Hindu Females		*Muslim Females*		*All Religion Females*	
	2001	*2011*	*2001*	*2011*	*2001*	*2011*
Secondary level/matric	5.6	7.3	3.9	5.5	5.6	7.2
Higher secondary	2.7	5.4	1.6	3.9	2.7	5.3
Technical or non-technical diploma or degree	0.2	0.3	0.1	0.3	0.2	0.3
Graduate and above	2.5	4.6	1.0	2.1	2.4	4.4
% with education secondary level and above	11.0	17.6	6.6	11.8	10.9	17.2
	Hindu M + F		*Muslim M + F*		*All Religion M +F*	
	2001	*2011*	*2001*	*2011*	*2001*	*2011*
Secondary level/matric	7.7	9.0	5.3	6.3	7.7	8.7
Higher secondary	3.7	6.6	2.2	4.4	3.7	6.4
Technical or non-technical diploma or degree	0.4	0.7	0.2	0.4	0.4	0.7
Graduate and above	3.7	6.0	1.7	2.8	3.7	5.6
% with education secondary level and above	15.5	22.3	9.4	13.9	15.5	21.4

according to the 2011 data only under 18 per cent Hindu and 12 per cent Muslim women in their respective total population had completed secondary level education and beyond, the decadal increase was faster among the Muslim women compared to Hindu women.[11] There indeed is a realization to educate daughters among the Muslims. In order to understand whether higher level of education will enable Muslim girls to plan their families and not succumb to pressures from others to bear several children, it is important to examine the role of other factors and their interaction with religion. One unit level analysis based on the NFHS–1 and NFHS–2 data by Bhat and Zavier (2005) is quite cautious in interpreting the results from their statistical analysis. They find that even after controlling for all the known socio-economic factors, religion emerges as a significant factor explaining fertility level in both rural and urban areas. They find that the religion effect does not disappear at higher level of education; in fact, the Hindu–Muslim differences in ideal family size become wider as the level of education increases.

It is tempting to attribute the residual effect of religion to the precepts and theology of Islam. It is often argued that Islam is against contraception and its interpreters preach that children are gifts of God and should be accepted by all practising the religion regardless of their socio-economic status or other compulsions. In a field-based small study undertaken in Karnataka state, Iyer (2002b) noted that 40 per cent of ever married Muslim women in her study sample reported to have ever used any method of contraception as against 57 per cent of Hindu women. Also, Muslim women had given birth to an average of 3.7 children as against 2.7 born to Hindu women. Thus, Muslim women had higher fertility and lower contraceptive use compared to the Hindu women, supporting the popular perception. She therefore tested the pure religion effect by seeking information on the belief systems of both the religious groups and also by collecting information on the characteristics of all the women to test whether the effect of religion remains significant after controlling the effect of all other factors such as woman's education, husband's education, household income, occupation of both woman and her husband, woman's current age, her reported ease of access to government contraceptive services and so on.

When information was sought on how faithfully women practiced their religion, role of the religious leaders in their lives, and how often they prayed, it was noted that religion was far more important in the lives of Muslim women compared to in the day-to-day life of Hindu women. Muslim women also thought that their religion did not permit use of contraception. However, in spite of the differences in the reported importance of religion among Hindus and Muslims, when the effect of various socioeconomic characteristics was controlled, there was no statistically significant difference between Hindus and Muslims in the effect of religion on contraceptive adoption. Evidently, the inferences drawn by Iyer based on a small study are not supported by a regression-based decomposition exercise using data from a large randomly drawn national sample as demonstrated by Bhat and Zavier (2005).

Admittedly, Karnataka is among the better-developed states, where, as shown above in Table 2.6, the Hindu–Muslim differences in TFR (2.1 for Hindus as against 2.2 for Muslims in 2005–2006) and contraceptive use rate (61% for Hindus and 56% for Muslims in 2005–2006) are narrower compared to that in some of the core North Indian states such as Bihar. What the state level data and micro-study of Iyer show and substantiate is that Muslims are limiting their families when others around them are also doing that; in fact doing at a faster pace. On the other hand, based on several years of ethnographic in-depth research in a district of Uttar Pradesh, Jeffery and Jeffery (2005) had observed that those 'Muslims who have experienced more schooling, are wealthier and live in towns have lower fertility than those with less schooling, poorer and rural'. But importantly, this applies to their other neighbouring non-Muslim population groups as well. Their argument for the differentials along socio-economic class goes beyond such simplified categories. Micro-level data enable them to observe that Hindus and Muslims in spite of living in the same area are differentially placed in structures of power and influence with very different effects on fertility and the role of state or what Jeffery and Jeffery call 'governmentality' in post-independent India has become important in creating differential access to the benefits that the state provides.

A micro-level qualitative study of Muslim women with different educational background in India and Bangladesh undertaken by Sahu and Hutter (2012) noted that Muslim women in both the countries are not passive followers of religion norms but have agency to take charge of their lives and play active role in planning their family. In India, Muslim women accept sterilization, sometimes without the knowledge of their family members and make a flexible interpretation of Islam when they take reproductive decisions. The messages from the in-depth ethnographic studies are loud and clear. There is a need to provide health and family planning services taking into account the needs and preferences of people at the local level including religious needs.

The access to health services is of importance even with regard to basic vaccination to Muslim children. While infant and child mortality has been lowered among Muslims compared to that among Hindus that has been observed historically and by most researchers, the per cent of children protected against all childhood illnesses by immunization is lower among Muslims compared to other religious groups as shown in Table 2.13. All the three NFHS have shown that with the case of the three doses of DPT vaccine, measles vaccine and oral polio. It is important to find out whether the services are less utilized by the Muslims or are less available to the Muslim households and whether the service providers during their field visits do not contact or inform certain households. It has been sometimes argued that in rural areas women who are engaged in casual work do not always know or are not present when their young children are given vaccination and children receive vaccination in the presence of some other older sibling or child's caretaker. However, available data show that a very small per cent of Muslim women are engaged in paid work outside their homes

Table 2.13 *Immunization Status of Children by Religion, NFHS–1, NFHS–2 and NFHS–3*

Religion	NFHS–1 (1992–1993)				NFHS–2 (1998–1999)				NFHS–3 (2005–2006)			
	BCG	DPT3	Polio3	Measles	BCG	DPT3	Polio3	Measles	BCG	DPT3	Polio3	Measles
Hindu	63.3	53.1	54.6	42.9	72.5	55.7	63.5	51.5	76.9	56.4	78.7	60.0
Muslim	51.2	38.1	41.5	32.3	62.3	45.7	54.0	40.4	69.7	47.8	76.6	49.6
Christian	70.7	60.3	60.6	50.0	84.0	72.8	76.5	66.2	82.1	65.1	77.6	68.0
Sikh	79.8	72.0	73.2	64.7	86.4	77.6	80.5	75.7	90.4	76.9	81.1	80.2
Total	62.2	51.7	53.4	42.2	71.6	55.1	62.8	50.7	78.1	55.3	78.2	58.8

compared to other groups and therefore this argument has a different connotation for different communities.

Conclusion

The various data presented do unequivocally establish the fact that the fear that Muslims will become majority in India is completely baseless and passion aroused by some zealous and fanatical demagogues must at best be ignored. The reality is that fertility of Muslims has started falling, desire for many children is weakening, contraceptive use is increasing and need for family planning is growing. These facts cannot be ignored or overlooked. As late entrants to demographic transition, Muslims have been catching up at faster pace in reducing their fertility and increasing the use of family planning methods. The gap especially between Hindus and Muslims is narrowing throughout the country. In the demographically advanced states, the levels of Muslim fertility is only marginally higher than the Hindu fertility. The gap in educational attainment of women between the two communities has been narrowing and it is very unlikely that educated Muslim women desire several children. They are no different from other women similarly placed with regard to providing their children good education and better living standards. No population group, including Indian Muslims, can remain unaffected by the winds of change.

At the same time, it must be recognized that not only the right-wing extremist Hindus, but also policymakers and researchers treat Muslim community as one monolith group, while admitting and studying the diversity within the Hindu community. There are notable differences within the Indian Muslim community as well; they speak languages of the regions they reside in and emulate the behaviour or even compete with the members of the dominant group in pursuit of education, vocation and so on. It would be of immense importance to study the characteristics of various subgroups within the Muslim community and how the subgroups are responding to the socio-economic changes sweeping across the country and how flexibly they interpret religion precepts affecting their daily lives.

Also, Indian Muslims cannot remain immune to the globalized world and to how the Muslims elsewhere are responding to the all-pervasive winds of change. Iran, a Muslim country, in a very short span has reduced its fertility below replacement level. With a population that is more than 90 per cent Muslim, Bangladesh has a TFR not only lower than India's overall TFR but also lower than that of Hindus in several states of India. The transition to smaller family compared to the past is evident everywhere. Eventually TFR in India also will hover around replacement level and no population group or religious group is unlikely to behave differently.

Notes

1. The Indian censuses or the large national-level surveys ask the question on religion of the person or household head in terms of affiliation or self-reporting of belonging to a certain religion. Questions on actual participation in terms of attendance at place of worship or praying or on belief system and practices that reflect religion, important as they are, are not canvassed in surveys. This chapter is largely based on religious affiliation as identified by the respondents.
2. In fact, after the results of 2001 Census were released to the public, data on religion distribution generated a huge controversy and heated debate in media and among scholars because the census organization inadvertently did not adjust the decadal growth rate of Muslims taking into account the fact that in Jammu & Kashmir the 1991 Census was not conducted.
3. It has been alleged that the UPA government took a decision not to release the religious data ahead of the Lok Sabha election in 2014 that would arouse communal tension and face a resurgent BJP party.
4. The projections made about the number of Hindus and Muslims in India by 2050, by Pew Research Center, a non-profit, non-partisan fact tank, based in Washington, D.C.,

United States, have received a lot of media attention in India and are widely quoted to show that Muslims will constitute 18.4 per cent of India's total population by 2050. Their projections are based on the available data from the censuses and the National Family Health Surveys with the assumptions that the observed trends in fertility and mortality will continue in future (See: Pew Research Center, 2015, *The Future of World Religions: Population Growth Projections, 2010--2050*). However, a few Hindu Right-wing extremists have gone further to proclaim that Muslims will eventually become majority in India because according to them Islam allows polygyny, widow remarriage and advocates unrestricted procreation resulting in high fertility.

5. Needless to add that Indians did not always perceive themselves as belonging to a particular religious group and so the British Census commissioners had difficulties delineating or assigning religion to people on the basis of their reported social or cultural practices, caste affiliation or occupation. The boundary line between Hindus on the one hand and Sikhs or Jains on the other, for example, was often found to be indeterminate (See: Bhagat, 2013, on religious identity problems in India).
6. The 2001 Census Operation took a bold decision to make available in public domain data on age distribution, level of education and occupation for all the major religious groups. The practice has continued in 2011.
7. According to the family planning survey conducted by Operations Research Group, Baroda, the contraceptive prevalence rate in 1970 was estimated to be 14 per cent for the country as a whole.
8. When the data from the NFHS–4, conducted during 2015–2016 or a decade after the third NFHS, become available on fertility experience and contraceptive use of women by their socio-economic characteristics, including religion, the pace or the momentum of transition would become clearer.
9. The education level data for the major religious groups from the Census of India were made available for the first time since independence in 2001 and the practice has continued with the

2011 Census as well. The latter were released only towards the end of August 2016.

10. The narrowing of gender differentials implies that the proportion of educated men marrying illiterate women would decrease. Also, educated women would be better placed in terms of asserting some autonomy vis-à-vis their husbands and in-laws.
11. For majority of the newspapers, the interesting story line from the recently released 2011 Census data on the level of educational attainment by the religious groups was that there were only 5.6 per cent Indians with education level of graduation and above. Among Hindus, this percentage was 6, whereas among Muslims it was only 2.7 or less than half of what was noted among Hindus. The Jains were the group with 26 per cent of its followers having attained this high level of education. Hardly any newspapers commented on the narrowing of differentials over time among all, but more so among Muslims compared to other religious groups (See national dailies of September 1 and 2, 2016.)

References

Alagrajan, M. and P. Kulkarni, 2005. 'Population Growth, Fertility, and Religion in India', *Economic and Political Weekly*, Vol. 40, No. 5, January 29, pp. 403–10.

Bhagat, R.B. 2013. 'Census Enumeration, Religious Identity and Communal Polarization in India', *Asian Ethnicity*, Vol. 14, No. 4, pp. 434–48.

Bhat, P.N. Mari, 1996. 'Contours of Fertility Decline in India: A District Level Study Based on the 1991 Census', in Srinivasan, K. (ed.), *Population Policy and Reproductive Health*, Delhi: Hindustan Publishing Corporation, pp. 96–180.

Bhat, P.N. Mari and A.J.F. Zavier, 2005. 'Role of Religion in Fertility Decline: The Case of Indian Muslims', *Economic and Political Weekly*, Vol. 40, No. 5, January 29, pp. 385–402.

Bongaarts, J. 1978. 'A Framework for Analysing the Proximate Determinants of Fertility', *Population and Development Review*, Vol. 4, No. 1, pp. 105–32.

Bose, A. 2005. 'Beyond Hindu-Muslim Growth Rates: Understanding Socio-economic Reality', *Economic and Political Weekly*, Vol. 40, No. 5, January 29, pp. 370–4.

Dharmalingam, A. and S. Philip Morgan, 2004. 'Pervasive Muslim-Hindu Fertility Differences in India', *Demography*, 41(3), pp. 528–545.

Dharmalingam, A., K. Kavaneetham and S.P. Morgan, 2005, 'Hindu-Muslim Fertility Differences: Evidence from National Family Health Survey-II', *Economic and Political Weekly*, Vol. 40, No. 5, January 29, 99. 429–36.

International Institute for Population Sciences (IIPS), 1995. National Family Health Survey (MCH and Family Planning), India, 1992–1993, Bombay: IIPS.

International Institute for Population Sciences (IIPS) and ORC Macro, 2000. National Family Health Survey (NFHS–2), 1998–1999: India, Mumbai: IIPS.

International Institute for Population Sciences (IIPS) and Macro International, 2007. National Family Health Survey (NFHS–3), 2005–2006: India, Vols. 1 and 2, Mumbai: IIPS.

Iyer, Sriya, 2002a. *Demography and Religion in India*, New Delhi: Oxford University Press.

Iyer, Sriya, 2002b. 'Understanding Religion and the Economics of Fertility in India', published as *Centre of South Asia Studies Occasional Paper 2*, Cambridge: Centre of South Asia Studies.

James, K.S. and S.B. Nair, 2005. 'Accelerated Decline in Fertility in India Since the 1980s: Trends among Hindus and Muslims', *Economic and Political Weekly*, Vol. 40, No. 5, January 29, pp. 375–83.

Jeffery, R. and P. Jeffery, 2005. 'Saffron Demography, Common Wisdom, Aspirations and Uneven Governmentalities', *Economic and Political Weekly*, Vol. 40, No. 5, January 29, pp. 447–53.

McQuillan, K. 2004. 'When Does Religion Influence Fertility?', *Population and Development Review*, Vol. 30, No. 1 pp. 25–56.

Mishra, V. 2004. 'Muslim/Non-Muslim Differentials in Fertility and Family Planning in India', East-West Center Working Papers, Population and Health Series No. 112, January.

Pew Research Center, 2015. *The Future of World Religions: Population Growth Projections, 2010–2050*; Also, *By 2050, India to Have World's Largest Populations of Hindus and Muslims,* Released on April 21 by Pew Research Center, Fact Tank: Our Lives in Numbers, Washington, DC.

SRS. 1984. *Fertility Differentials in India,* 1989, New Delhi: Registrar General of India.

Rajan, S.I. 2005. 'District Level Fertility Level Estimates for Hindus and Muslims', *Economic and Political Weekly,* Vol. 40, No. 5, January 29, pp. 437–46.

Reddy, P.H. 2003, 'Religion, Population Growth, Fertility and Family Planning Practices in India', *Economic and Political Weekly,* Vol. 38, No. 33, August 16, pp. 3500–9.

Sahu, B. and I. Hutter, 2012. "Lived Islam' in India and Bangladesh: Negotiating Religion to Realize Reproductive Aspirations', *Culture, Health and Sexuality,* Vol. 14, No. 5, pp. 521–35.

Visaria, L. and P. Visaria. 1982. 'Population in the Indian Subcontinent, 1957–1947', in Meghnad Desai and Dharma Kumar (eds.), *The Cambridge Economic History of India Volume II,* Cambridge: Cambridge University Press, 1982.

3 Transition in Hindu and Muslim Population Growth Rates

Myth and Reality

R.B. Bhagat

Demography has acquired a centre stage in India's contemporary politics. While on the one hand, the potential of demographic dividend is extolled as a means to scale up India as a global economic power, on the other hand, religious differentials in population growth rates are being raised to the level of demographic anxiety evoking communal polarization and tension. The emergence of the field of demography is crucially linked with the appearance of the census in many countries of Europe during the eighteenth century, which helps us to understand the relationship between population, territory and state (Bhagat 2013). With transition and strengthening of democracy, census expanded in many Western countries in its scope and content. However, care was taken to keep aside the controversial issues of religion and ethnicity. The British census incorporated a question on religion in 2001 census after a strong pressure to include ethnicity in 1991 census (Bhagat 2003; Peach 2000). On the other hand, a judicious application of census was not seen in the countries under the colonial rule. As a result, the demographic statistics generated along religion and caste lines were turned out to be a means to widen communal and caste polarizations at the political level. On the other hand, census also showed that India has been a country hugely diverse and plural in the past. In colonial census when caste was recorded, the number of castes were as high as 4,147 (Bhagat 2006). Census also reported as many as 1,700 religious groups which were codified in the 2001 census, but data was not published. Demographic data by religion was published only for six major religions of India namely, Hindus, Muslims, Christians, Sikhs, Buddhists and Jains. A large number of small religious groups and faiths were kept under the category of 'Others' (Census of India 2001).

In independent India, there has been an effort to suppress caste data by not collecting the correct information except the SCs and STs. On the contrary, there was no interference to the British legacy on the census of religious groups. As such in each census just after the release of data on religion, there was a heightened concern on the religious demography of India. It is ironical that while on the one hand, there is euphoria about the demographic dividend, on the other there are passions flared up on the relative growth rates of different religious communities.

One of the first reactions arose at the beginning of the twentieth century when the 1901 census revealed a decline in the growth rate of Hindu population. This led to an articulation of a demographic theory of Hindus as a dying race (Mukherji 1909). The fear of Hindus being outnumbered has since then erupted after almost every census. Concerns have been raised that a higher fertility among Muslims is essentially rooted in Islam and that Muslim men can have four wives. It has been clarified that Islam is not against family planning (Khan 1978; Tantawi 1988) and that polygamy is not necessarily related to high fertility. On the contrary, it is found that women in polygamous marriages have lower fertility (Bongaarts, Frank and Lesthaeghe 1984). Furthermore, it is also not true that the prevalence of polygamous marriages is higher among Muslims compared to Hindus (Census of India 1971). E.A. Gait, the Census Commissioner of 1911 census, had observed almost a century ago, 'a Muhammadan may have four wives, but he also in practice is generally monogamous. As a rule, it is only the comparatively rich who indulge in the luxury, if such it should prove, of a second wife' (1913: 246).

Several earlier studies have shown that Muslim fertility and population growth has been higher than Hindus due to many reasons such as low education and economic status, lack of access to health services and higher unmet need for family planning, and also a time lag in the onset of fertility decline (Bhagat and Praharaj 2005). Muslim communities in India also do not show a homogeneous pattern in the level of fertility and population growth rates across states. For instance, Muslims in Kerala show lower fertility and population growth than Hindus of Uttar Pradesh. There are many such instances indicating the fact that India's demographic reality is far more regional than the religious differences per se producing it. This chapter throws light on the above-mentioned aspects of the differentials in Hindu–Muslim population growth rates and their transitions in the light of 2011 census data.

Emerging Scenario after 2011 Census

After independence, the population data by religion are hugely affected by mass migration, so a comparison of population growth since 1961 would be more appropriate. Figure 3.1 shows that Muslim population was enumerated at 46.9 million compared to 366.5 million of Hindus in 1961. These figures increased to 172.2 million among Muslims and 966.2 million among Hindus in 2011.

When the Census of India released the population data by religion in the month of August 2015, the national daily such as *Times of India* published the breaking news such as Muslim population grew by 0.8 per cent, and Hindu population declined by 0.7 per cent in the front page (*Times of India*, August 25, 2015). It created an impression among many including a TV channel that called the author to know why Hindu population has declined, which was not true.

India's population grew by 182 million during 2001–2011 out of which 138 million was contributed by Hindus and 34 million by Muslims, that is, four times higher among Hindus in an absolute sense compared to Muslims. It is also a fact that no major religious community in India has declined in absolute numbers as per data released by 2011 census. However, statistics is a good servant but could be a bad master. The media took up the statistics as shown in Table 3.1 that the proportion of Hindu population which stood at 80.5 per cent in 2001 declined to 79.8 per cent, that is, a decline in share by 0.7 per cent, whereas the share of Muslim population increased from 13.4 to 14.2 per cent – an increase of 0.7 per cent.

Figure 3.1 *Population Trend among Hindus and Muslims, 1961–2011*

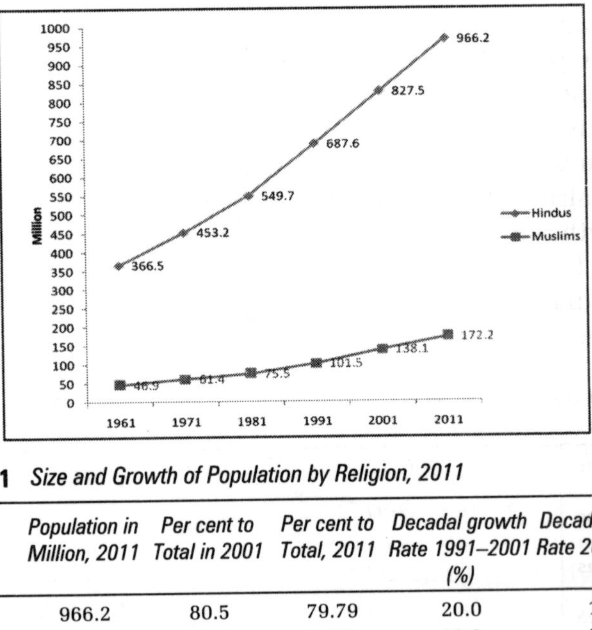

Table 3.1 *Size and Growth of Population by Religion, 2011*

Religious Group	Population in Million, 2011	Per cent to Total in 2001	Per cent to Total, 2011	Decadal growth Rate 1991–2001 (%)	Decadal growth Rate 2001–2011 (%)
Hindus	966.2	80.5	79.79	20.0	16.8
Muslim	172.2	13.4	14.22	29.3	24.6
Christians	27.8	2.3	2.29	22.1	15.5
Sikh	20.8	1.9	1.72	16.9	8.4
Buddhist	8.4	0.8	0.69	23.2	6.1
Jain	4.4	0.4	0.36	26.0	5.3
Others*	7.9	0.6	0.65	11.3	19.5
Total	1,210.8	100	100	21.5	17.7

*Others do not include religion not stated comprising 2.86 million in 2011 compared to 0.72 million in 2001.

Source: Census of India (2001); For 2011 Census Data, see www.censusindia.gov.in.

However, it is also a fact that the growth rate of Muslim community has been declining since 1980s. Figure 3.2 shows that Hindu growth rate peaked during 1971–1981 depicting a decadal growth rate of 24.2 per cent, whereas the Muslim growth rate peaked during 1981–1991 at the decadal growth rate of 32.9 per cent. It may be deduced from Figure 3.2 that there is a time lag of about 10 years in the onset of demographic transition between the two communities. The theory of demographic transition informs us that all communities and regions are likely to pass through demographic transition ultimately reaching to a stationary population (zero population growth) (Lee 2003). However, this will depend upon mostly on the timing of the onset of fertility decline and also the pace of fertility decline. As different communities start with different timings of fertility decline, and also differ in pace, the year by which zero population growth will be reached is likely to differ depending on the time lag. Looked from this perspective, Muslim community of India is not an exception and the population stabilization is inevitable as evident from the decline in population

Figure 3.2 *Decadal Growth Rate of Hindus and Muslims, 1961 to 2011*

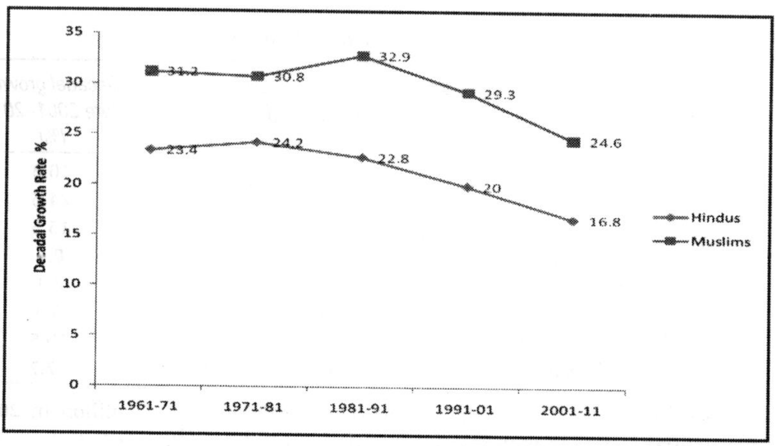

Note: Adjusted growth rate as census was not held in Assam in 1981 and in Jammu and Kashmir in 1991.

growth transitions among Muslim which started in the 1980s compared with Hindus in the 1970s. As the demographic transition is fundamentally linked to the process of development and modernization particularly through the routes of expansion of education and rising urbanization, socio-economic differentials among religious groups are very important to understand the relative population growth and differentials among them.

Table 3.2 *Socio-economic Indicators among Hindus and Muslims, India, 2001 and 2011*

Indicators	*Hindus*		*Muslims*		*All Religions*	
	2001	*2011*	*2001*	*2011*	*2001*	*2011*
Level of Urbanization (%)	26.1	29.2	35.7	39.9	27.8	31.1
Literacy Rate (%)						
Male	76.2	81.6	67.6	74.7	75.3	80.8
Female	53.2	64.3	50.1	62.0	53.7	64.6
Total	65.1	73.2	59.1	68.5	64.8	72.9
Work Participation Rate (%)						
Male	52.4	53.9	47.5	49.5	51.7	53.2
Female	27.5	27.3	14.1	14.7	25.6	25.5
Total	40.4	41.0	31.3	32.5	39.1	39.7
% of workers in						
Agriculture	60.7	57.0	42.7	40.5	58.2	56.6
Household Industry	3.8	6.8	8.1	13.9	4.2	7.6
Others	35.5	36.2	49.1	45.6	37.6	35.8
Sex ratio (F/M) per 1,000	931	939	936	951	933	942
Child Sex Ratio (F/M) per 1,000	925	913	950	942	927	918
% of Population 0–6 to Total Population	15.6	13.1	18.7	16.4	15.9	13.5

Source: Same as in Table 3.1.

Table 3.2 presents socio-economic indicators of Hindus and Muslims for the census years 2001 and 2011. A higher proportion of Muslims lives in urban areas (about 40%) compared to 29 per cent of Hindus. Also, the literacy rate among Muslims is found to be lower than Hindus and that of the national average. While the difference between the average literacy rate of India and Muslims was 4 per cent, it is much wider (about 6%) between Hindus and Muslims. Further, the gap in literacy rates remains more or less similar during 2001 and 2011. Table 3.2 also shows lower work participation rates among Muslims compared to the average of India as well as Hindus. It is worthwhile to note that Muslim women show half the work participation compared to Hindus. Being more urban based, a higher percentage of Muslims are engaged in non-agricultural activities. However, in urban areas most of the Muslim workforce is self-employed. On the other hand, regular salaried workers are one of the lowest among Muslims (Basant 2012). Also, they lag much behind in both education and employment levels as compared to all India level and Hindus. However, in respect to sex ratios (female/male), Muslims show a better position of women compared to Hindus and all India average (see Table 3.2).

Regional Variations in Muslim Population Growth

It is generally believed that Muslims are a homogenous group which is not true. Diversity in terms of ethnicity, caste, language, cultural practices and food are very much evident among Muslims. Apart from differences between *Shia* and *Sunni* based on faith and practices, Muslims are also broadly divided into *Ashrafs* and *Ajlafs*. Ashrafs are the noble sections that trace their origin from foreign immigrants and consist of Sayyad, Shaik, Moghul and Pathan. The Ajlaf groups are mainly the converts and constitute several occupation groups – such as *Julaha* (weaver), *Darzi* (tailor), *Qassab* (butcher), *Nai* or *Hajjam* (barber), *Mirasi* (musician) and *Bhangi* (sweeper) (Ansari 1959; Ahmad 1978). It will also not be correct to associate exclusively the language of *Urdu* to Muslims (Basant 2007). On the other hand, Muslims speak regional languages such as Marathi, Gujarati, Bengali, Tamil and Malayalam with as much fervour and belongingness as Hindus or any other religious group in our regional settings.

Table 3.3 *Size, Distribution and Growth of Muslim Population, India and States, 2011*

Sr.No.	*State*	*Muslim Population*	*% Muslim to State Population*	*% to India's Muslim Population*	*Decadal Growth Rate 2001–2011 (%)*
1	Jammu and Kashmir	8,567,485	68.3	4.97	26.1
2	Himachal Pradesh	149,881	2.2	0.08	25.4
3	Uttarakhand	1,406,825	13.9	0.81	39.9
4	Punjab	535,489	5.3	0.31	40.1
5	Haryana	1,781,342	7.0	1.03	45.6
6	Delhi	2,158,684	12.9	1.25	32.9
7	Rajasthan	6,215,377	9.1	3.60	29.8
8	Uttar Pradesh	38,483,967	19.3	22.34	25.1
9	Bihar	17,557,809	16.9	10.19	27.9
10	Assam	10,679,345	34.3	6.2	29.5
11	West Bengal	24,654,825	27.0	14.2	21.8
12	Jharkhand	4,793,994	14.5	2.78	28.4
13	Orissa	911,670	2.2	0.52	19.6
14	Chhattisgarh	514,998	2.0	0.29	25.7
15	Madhya Pradesh	4,774,695	6.6	2.77	24.2
16	Gujarat	5,846,761	9.7	3.99	27.3
17	Maharashtra	12,971,152	11.5	7.53	26.2
18	Andhra Pradesh + Telangana	8,082,412	9.5	4.69	15.6
19	Karnataka	7,893,065	12.9	4.58	22.1
20	Goa	121,564	8.3	0.07	31.8
21	Kerala	8,873,472	26.6	5.15	12.8
22	Tamil Nadu	4,229,479	5.9	2.45	21.8
23	Rest	1,040,867	2.9	0.60	27.1

Source: Census of India (2011), see www.censusindia.gov.in.

Dyson and Moore (1983) observed that the regional features outweigh religious ones as Hindu and Muslims show more similarity with each other within the regional demographic regimes than they do with co-religionists elsewhere in the subcontinent. However, in contrast to the scientific reality, diversity among Muslim society is rarely recognized (Basant 2007). Table 3.3 shows that Jammu and Kashmir is the only state with a majority of Muslims (68%), but comprises only about 5 per cent of India's population. The four states namely Uttar Pradesh, Bihar, West Bengal and Assam comprise about half of the Muslim population of the country. This reflects that Muslim population is not only regionally concentrated but also belong to states which are underdeveloped. Outside this regional block, Kerala is the state where Muslims constitute one-fourth of the state's population, but this amounts to only 5 per cent of the India's Muslim population. Thus, the numerical presence in the respective states and India as a whole are two different aspects so far the condition of Muslims is concerned. It was noted in the earlier section that Muslim population growth rate at all India level has been declining since the 1980s with a decadal growth rate of 24.6 per cent observed during 2001–2011. It is also worthwhile to note from Table 3.3 that the population growth rate of Muslims in many states namely West Bengal, Orissa, Kerala, Andhra Pradesh (including Telangana) and Tamil Nadu show lower population growth rate compared to the national average. Thus, the demographic behaviour of Muslim is not uniform across states of India. When Hindus of Bihar and Uttar Pradesh are compared with Muslims of Kerala, they have much higher growth rates. The decadal growth rate among Hindus in Bihar is double (24.6%) compared to growth rate of 12.8 per cent among Muslims in Kerala during 2001–2011. In Uttar Pradesh also, it is one-half times higher among Hindus (18.9%) compared to Muslims of Kerala. Muslims of Andhra Pradesh (including Telangana) also has shown a decadal growth rate of 15.6 per cent, that is, lower than the national growth rate of 16.8 per cent among Hindus during 2001–2011. These facts indicate that nothing is unique about Muslim population growth except to the existence of a delayed demographic transition.

Fertility Level among Muslims and Future Population Growth

Population growth among any social group is the result of fertility, mortality and migration. Out of these three components, fertility is more closely related to religion. Religion influences cultural norms and beliefs guiding reproductive behaviour. While it is true that most of the religions have been pronatalist, it has never been able to stall fertility decline and consequently the demographic transition. This is also true for Muslims across the world. Figure 3.3 shows that there are many Muslim majority countries which have lower fertility level than India. The fertility level across groups and regions is measured on the basis of TFR. TFR is the average number of children that would be born alive to a hypothetical cohort of women if, throughout their reproductive years, the age-specific fertility rates for the specified year remained unchanged. In short, it means the number of live births a woman is expected to bear during her entire reproductive life.

India shows TFR of 2.4 compared to 2.2 of Bangladesh and as low as 1.8 in Iran. TFR of Malaysia, Turkey and Tunisia is also lower than India. On the other hand, it is

Figure 3.3 *Total Fertility Rate of Some Muslim Majority Countries, 2013*

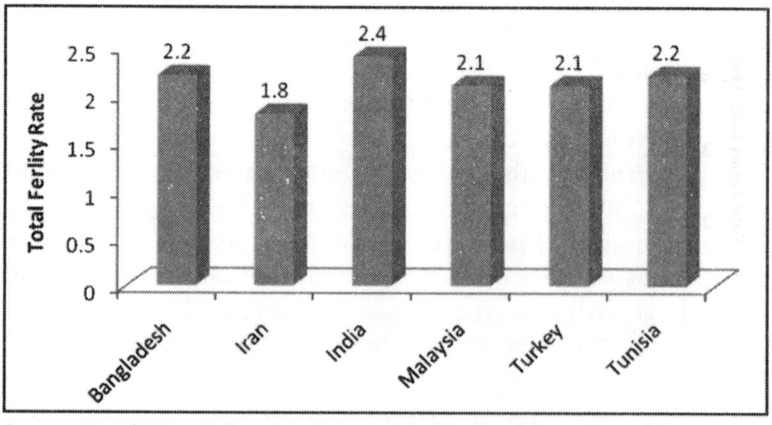

Source: Population Reference Bureau, World Population Data Sheet, 2014, Washington, DC (www.prb.org).

higher in Indonesia (2.6), Saudi Arabia (2.9) and Pakistan (3.8) in 2013 (Population Reference Bureau 2014). The socio-economic conditions and government's policy and programmes play a very important role in determining fertility level across Muslim majority countries. The Muslim societies across the world do not show stable levels of fertility. The spectacular fertility decline in Bangladesh and Iran provides good examples eroding the myth that Muslim society is resistant to adopting family planning and not amenable to fertility decline (Abbasi-Shavazi 2001; Das Gupta and Narayana 1997).

In India, Muslim fertility has been higher albeit with a difference of one child only during the decades 1980s and 1990s which was further reduced during the 2000s (see Figure 3.4). As per National Family Health Survey TFR among Hindus was 2.6 compared with 3 live births among Muslims. It may be also noted from Figure 3.4 that Muslim fertility has also substantially declined from about 6 live births in the early 1980s to 3 in the middle of the first decade

Figure 3.4 *Total Fertility Rate among Hindus and Muslims, 1984 to 2005–2006*

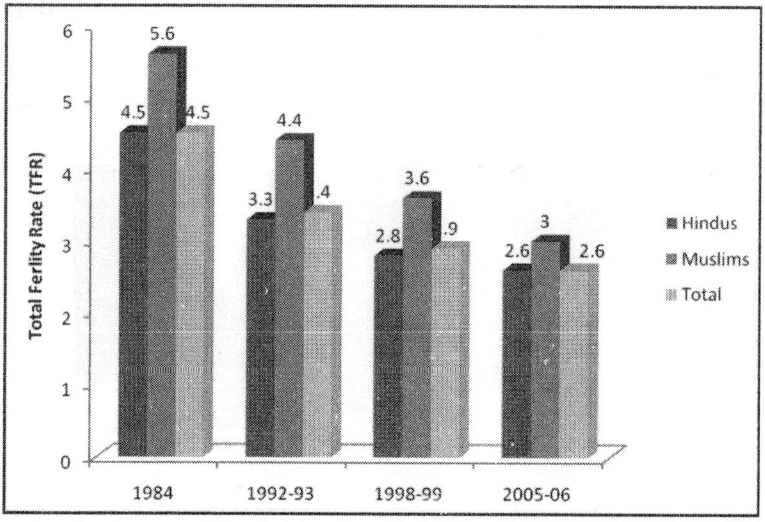

Source: Bhagat and Praharaj (2005) and International Institute for Population Sciences and Macro International (2007).

of the twenty-first century. A similar decline was also observed among Hindus but the level was lower (4.5 live births) during the early 1980s. This corroborates our earlier observation that the onset of fertility decline was earlier among Hindus, that is, almost a decade earlier than Muslims which will result in Muslims reaching replacement level of fertility almost a decade later. Thus, the demographic evidence shows that both communities are going to achieve population stabilization in the long run, although onset and pace of fertility decline differ considerably.

There are several arguments advanced relating religion to fertility. An argument of the 'particularized theology' says that it is the very essence of religion that influences fertility, irrespective of any socio-economic or demographic factors. On the other hand, others argue that fertility differentials are the outcome of differences in the socio-economic characteristics of the members of different religious groups. It is a well-established fact in the demographic literature that higher education leads to lower fertility, and this is true for Muslims as well (Alagarajan 2003; Bhagat and Praharaj 2005;

Figure 3.5 *Currently Married Women Using Contraceptive Methods among Hindus and Muslims, 2005–2006*

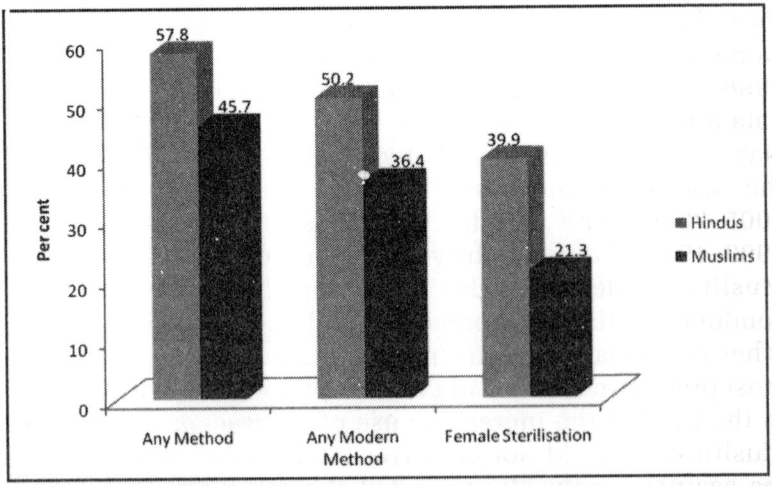

Source: International Institute for Population Sciences and Macro International (2007).

Bhat and Zavier 2005). Thus, it is not religion per se, but the characteristics of the religious groups that are important in influencing fertility levels (Chamei 1977). It is also argued that the minority status of a religious/ethnic group, which is more true in case of Indian Muslims as the community has experienced perpetual incidences of riots, can engender social and psychological insecurities, leading to the persistence of pronatalist attitude among them (Chattopadhyay, Bhagat and Roy 2004). However, the National Family Health Survey showed that only 2 per cent of women oppose the use of family planning on the ground of religion (International Institute for Population Sciences and Macro 2000).

There are many Islamic scholars who believe that Islam is not against family planning (Khan 1978; Tantawi 1988). The past and recent Islamic jurists (*Faqihs*) have mentioned some of the reasons that permit married couples to plan their families. These include to keep away from illegal income, protecting the health of wife and to provide children all material and spiritual needs. There is a *Hadith* which says that it is better to leave your children rich than leave them poor like beggars (Tantawi 1988).

The use of modern methods of family planning in India has been increasing rapidly among Indian Muslim women from 22 per cent in 1992–1993 to 30.2 per cent in 1998–1999 and 36.2 per cent in 2005–2006 for which latest data are available from NFHS. Figure 3.5 shows that there was a gap of 13.8 per cent between Hindus and Muslims in the use of modern methods of family planning in 2005–2006. The similar gap was 15.7 per cent in 1992–1993, that is, slightly narrowed down in 2005–2006. Muslim couples use higher level of spacing methods (pills, condom and IUD) compared to Hindus. However, like any other religious groups in India, female sterilization is the most predominant form of contraceptive use (21.3%). Also, in the light of the increasing use of contraceptives among Muslims, it would not be correct to assume that Muslims are against family planning. On the other hand, we also find that there is a high unmet need of family planning among them (19%) compared to Hindus (12%). The unmet need for both spacing methods (such as condom, IUD and pill) and terminal methods (sterilization) is higher among Muslims than Hindus. It is therefore evident that the demand for family planning among Muslims is less satisfied (International Institute for Population Sciences and Macro International 2007). Further, more Muslims than Hindus get family planning services from private sources (Mishra 2004). This raises an important question about the responsibility of the state in making the family planning services accessible to the larger Muslim population.

Population growth is not only the result of births but also deaths and migration. Although death rate is not available by religion, the existing evidence shows that Muslims have lower infant and child mortality rate (International Institute for Population Sciences and Macro International 2007). Bhat and Zavier (2005) estimated that life expectancy among Muslims is one year higher and death rate is 13 per cent lower compared to Hindus. Thus, it is quite important to emphasize that lower mortality among Muslims also contributed to the higher natural increase among them compared to Hindus. So far the cross border migration is concerned we do not have definite data on this aspect, although it is considered to be a burning issue for the state of Assam. Demographic evidences, however, do not support a high level of immigration at the all-India level (Bhagat 1998).

In spite of India achieving the replacement level of fertility (i.e., TFR 2.1) very soon, the population growth will continue for several decades due to demographic momentum triggered by young population and almost universal marriage practices. Table 3.4 shows that population of India will stabilize at the end of twenty-first century with Hindus constituting 1,270 million and Muslims 320 million population. The total population of the country will stabilize at about 1.7 billion.

Table 3.4 *Population Projection among Hindus and Muslims by 2101*

Year	*Population Projection (in million)*		
	Hindus	*Muslims*	*% Muslims*
2011 (Actual)	966	172	14.2
2021	1,060	210	15.4
2031	1,140	240	16.1
2041	1,210	260	16.7
2051	1,250	280	17.3
2061	31,270	300	17.8
2071	1,280	310	18.2
2081	1,270	310	18.6
2091	1,270	320	18.8
2101	1,270	320	18.8

Source: For projected population since 2021, see Bhat and Zavier (2005).

Thus, the percentage of Muslim population in India which was 14 per cent in 2011 would rise to about 18 per cent at the end of the twenty-first century as a result of time lag in demographic transition among Muslim community. So, while some rise in the share of Muslim population in the country is inevitable, it is no way going to outnumber Hindus as generally misconceived and conjectured in certain political circles.

Conclusions

The population growth and fertility level among Muslims has been relatively higher than Hindus, but showing a substantial declining trend. It is also not correct to presume that Muslims are a monolithic group as they are exhibiting varying levels of population growth and fertility levels. The decadal growth rate Muslim population varies as low as 10 to 15 per cent in the state of Kerala and undivided Andhra Pradesh to about 30 per cent in the states of Assam and Bihar. While studies show that the differential in fertility by religion does persist, there are ample evidences to confirm that fertility declines as women's education rises. This is also true for Muslims. On the other hand, Muslim population growth is also the product of mortality advantages as mortality is lower among Muslims compared to Hindus. There is also a time lag in the onset of fertility decline. So while Hindu population will likely to stabilize by 2061, Muslims will stabilize by 2071. In this event, some rise in the share of Muslims is likely, but the idea that Muslims will outnumber Hindus is a myth.

Muslims community in India not only constitutes the largest minority religious group, but also lagging behind in educational achievement and regular salaried jobs. The Prime Minister's High Powered Committee, popularly known as The Sachar Committee, examined in-depth the socio-economic conditions of Muslims and recognized that Muslims face issues relating to identity, security and equity due to their low socio-economic conditions, and low access to government jobs and political representation (The Sachar Committee 2006). The theory of demographic transition informs us that the demographic condition is not independent of socio-economic and political conditions. In Indian context, the feeling of insecurity gets reinforced as a result of frequent Hindu–Muslim riots that the country has experienced during freedom struggle and also after independence. This has not only an impact on communal polarization but also on the reproductive behaviour, and access to and the use of reproductive health services including family planning. The time lag in demographic transition among Muslims reflects the impact of the combination of interacting factors which are both socio-economic and political rooted in the minority status of the community. However, Muslims are not very different from those faced by the poor and less educated but their response to such problems is likely to be influenced by the issues they face vis-à-vis identity, security and inclusiveness. The gap between Hindus and Muslims in fertility levels is the result of the time lag in demographic transition between the two communities and is a passing phase in the demographic history of India. However, it is nonetheless important to emphasize that the access to reproductive health services in

Muslim-dominated localities and their inclusion in the socio-economic and political process is essential for our population policy and health programmes in order to build a healthy and strong India.

References

Abbasi-Shavazi, M.J. 2001. 'The Fertility Revolution in Iran', *Population and Societies*. The Monthly Newsletter of INED, Paris, No. 373, November.

Ahmad, I. 1978. *Caste and Social Stratification among Muslims in India,* Delhi: Manohar Publications.

Alagarajan, M. 2003. 'An Analysis of Fertility Differentials by Religion in Kerala State: A Test of the Interaction Hypothesis', *Population Research and Policy Review,* Vol. 22, No. 5, pp. 557–74.

Ansari, G. 1959. *Muslim Castes in Uttar Pradesh*, Lucknow: An Ethnographic and Folk Culture Society.

Basant, R. 2007. 'Diversity among Indian Muslims', *Seminar*, 569 (http://www.india-seminar.com/2007/569/569_rakesh_basant.htm, accessed on 28 May, 2016).

Basant, Rakesh. 2012. 'Education and Employment among Muslims in India: An Analysis of Patterns and Trends', Working Paper No. 2012-09-03, Indian Institute of Management, Ahmedabad.

Bhagat, R.B. 1998. 'Recent Trends in Population Growth and Fertility Level among Muslims in Major States of India, 1981–91', in M.H. Qureshi (ed.), *Muslims in India Since Independence: A Regional Perspective*, New Delhi: Institute of Objective Studies, pp. 67–80.

Bhagat, R.B. 2003. 'Role of Census in Ethnic and Racial Construction: US, British and Indian Censuses', *Economic and Political Weekly*, February 22, pp. 686–91.

Bhagat, R.B. and Purujit Praharaj. 2005. 'Hindu-Muslim Fertility Differentials', *Economic and Political Weekly*, Vol. 40, No. 5, pp. 411–18.

Bhagat, R.B. 2006. 'Census and Caste Enumeration: British Legacy and Contemporary Practice', *Genus*, Vol. 62, No. 2, pp. 119–34.

Bhagat, R.B. 2013. 'Census Enumeration, Religious Identity and Communal Polarization in India', *Asian Ethnicity*, Vol. 14, No. 4, pp. 434–48.

Bhat, Mari and A.J. Francis Zavier. 2005. 'Role of Religion in Fertility Decline: The Case of Indian Muslims', *Economic and Political Weekly*, Vol. 40, No. 5, pp. 385–402.

Bongaarts, J., O. Frank and R. Lesthaeghe. 1984. 'The Proximate Determinants of Fertility in Sub-Saharan Africa', *Population and Development Review*, Vol. 10, No. 3, pp. 511–37.

Chamei, J. 1977. 'Religious Differentials in Fertility: Lebanon, 1971', *Population Studies*, Vol. 32, No. 2, pp. 365–82.

Chattopadhyay, Aparajita, R.B. Bhagat and T.K. Roy. 2004. 'Hindu-Muslim Fertility Differentials in India: A Study of Selected States', in T.K. Roy, M. Guruswamy and P. Arokiaswamy (eds.), *Population, Health and Development*, Jaipur: Rawat, pp. 137–56.

Census of India. 1971. 'Polygamous Marriages in India: A Survey', *Miscellaneous Studies*, Monograph No. 4, New Delhi: Registrar General and Census Commissioner.

Census of India. 2001. The *First Report on Religion*, New Delhi: Registrar General and Census Commissioner.

Das Gupta, M. and D. Narayana. 1997. 'Bangladesh's Fertility Decline from a Regional Perspective', *Genus*, Vol. 53, Nos. 3–4, pp. 101–28.

Dyson, T. and M. Moore. 1983. 'On Kinship Structure, Female Autonomy and Demographic Behaviour in India', *Population and Development Review*, Vol. 9, No. 1, pp. 35--60.

Gait, E.A. 1913. *India*, Volume 1, Part I: Report, Census of India 1911, Superintendent, Government Printing, Calcutta, India.

International Institute for Population Sciences and Macro. 2000. India: National Family Health Survey (NFHS–2), 1998–1999, Mumbai: IIPS.

International Institute for Population Sciences and Macro International. 2007. India: National Family Health Survey (NFHS–3), 2005–2006, Volume I, Mumbai: IIPS.

Khan, M.E. 1978. *Birth Control amongst Muslims in India*, New Delhi: Manohar Publications.

Lee, Ronald (2003) 'The Demographic Transition: Three Centuries of Fundamental Change', *Journal of Economic Perspectives*, Vol. 17, No. 4, pp. 167–90.

Mishra, Vinod. 2004. 'Muslim/Non-Muslim Differentials in Fertility and Family Planning in India', Working Paper, Honolulu: East-West Centre.

Mukherji, U.N. 1909. *Hindus: A Dying Race*, Calcutta: M. Bannerjee.

Peach, C. 2000. 'Discovering White Ethnicity and Parachuted Plurality', *Progress in Human Geography*, Vol. 24, No. 4, p. 623.

Population Reference Bureau. 2014. *World Population Data Sheet*, Washington, DC (www.prb.org).

Sachar Committee, Prime Minister's High Level Committee. 2006. *Social, Economic and Educational Status of the Muslim Community of India: A Report*, New Delhi: Cabinet Secretariat, Govt. of India.

Tantawi, M.S. 1988. 'Birth Planning and Religious Point of View', *Population Science*, Vol. 8, pp. 1–14.

4 Religion-Based Identity Politics in India Since 1947

M.S. Gill

With a population of 1.21 billion in 2011, India is highly diverse in ethnic, linguistic, religious and cultural terms. As per the 2011 census, Hindus constitute the largest share of population (79.8%) followed by Muslims (14.2%), Christians (2.3%), Sikhs (1.7%), Buddhists (0.7%), Jains (0.4%) and others (0.7%). Most of the religious communities stand divided into numerous castes and sub-castes. This is particularly true of the Hindus who have four main *varnas* and hundreds of subcastes, and other ethnicities. Besides, tribal population constitutes 8.6 per cent of the total population of the country. To cap it, there also exist large intergroup socio-economic disparities. Different parts of the country have quite different historical, linguistic, religious and cultural contours and memories as per their own distinct experiences in times past. No wonder, the country has about 2,000 ethnic groups and 645 indigenous tribes; as per the 2011 census, there are 122 languages. However, the number of languages in the country is much larger, but data regarding those are not available since the Census of India does not collect data on the languages spoken by fewer than 10,000 persons.

This large religious, ethnic, and regional diversity had coexisted with little intercommunity friction in the past until about the mid-nineteenth century. This happened since during that long historical period there was indifferent spatial mobility of people and almost all rural settlements functioned more or less in benign isolation from other settlements. The same was true of urban centres, particularly the smaller ones which comprised an overwhelming majority at that time. During that period ethnic and religious identities had their relevance largely in the settlements of residence only.

But sometime in the second half of the nineteenth century, this type of spatial isolation started slowly fading away owing to expansion of the information field of people due to the following factors: (i) gradual expansion of road- and rail-network in the country; (ii) beginning of the census enumerations in the second half of the nineteenth century that instigated interest in population numbers relative to the other communities; (iii) emergence of religious revivalist and reform movements, particularly in North India and (iv) beginning of the electoral process for the formation of governments in different parts of the country. Apart from widening their information fields, all these factors also led to gradual awakening of people, particularly the upper layer, about the wider implications of religious identities and their relevance to power politics of their respective communities. The allocation of separate quota of electoral seats to different religious communities prior to 1947 added further interest as well as stakes in the issue of religion-based identity. To cap it, the rise of the demand for Pakistan in the mid-1920s, and the partition of the country on the basis of religion in 1947 had pushed the issue of religion-based identity to the top in the politics of the subcontinent, at the time of the end of the British rule. In this way, 'the growth of nationalism in India was unfortunately accompanied by a parallel growth of communalism' (Habib 2015: xxxv).

Post-Independence Period

The independence of the country in 1947 was accompanied by widespread communal violence in northern part of the subcontinent and an unanticipated and unplanned transfer of about 10 million people across two sides of the then newly created border between India and Pakistan, and that too in a short span of a few weeks. The violence associated with this phenomenon had claimed tens of thousands of innocent lives. All this worked to strengthen religious identities of different communities across the country, particularly in and around areas that had witnessed widespread communal violence and forced exchange of population between the two countries in the wake of the partition of the subcontinent. One of the consequences of these events was rapid increase in the emphasis on religion-based identity along with various sorts of religious and ethnic othering.

The demand for, and later the creation of a Muslim country, Pakistan seems to have also encouraged the view that the remaining territory of the subcontinent is the land of Hindus. Some hints to this effect can be found even in the Constitution of the country at some places. Two examples would suffice here: first, the Article 25 (2) (b) of the Constitution says that the reference to 'Hindus shall be construed as including a reference to persons professing the Sikh, Jain or Buddhist religion, and the reference to Hindu religious institutions shall be construed accordingly'. Similarly Hindu Code Bill of 1955 also treats all these three religious groups as Hindu. In fact, 'it included anyone in the definition of a Hindu who was not a Muslim, Christian, Parsi or Jew' (Singh 2005: 916); and secondly, the use of the name 'Bharat' for India 'in the opening article was meant to suggest a sense of Hindu ownership of the new India – the India which was perceived to have achieved self-rule after many centuries of foreign rule' (Singh 2005: 911–12). Even reservation by castes ultimately gets limited to Hindus and those who are not Muslim, Christian, Parsi or Jew.

It is generally the case that the promotion of religious identity also involves roping in religious faiths of relatively smaller or marginal religious communities with identities lesser known to the modern world. This has been done by almost every majority religious community in different countries. India is no exception to this practice. The first census of religion in post-independence India in 1961 categorized large number of tribal communities traditionally affiliated to dozens of different faiths in central India as Hindus which at the time of 1931 census were listed under the title 'tribal religions'. It is not fully clear as to why tribal people have been reclassified as Hindus; either they were considered, in the words of Ghurye (1963: 19), as 'backward Hindus', or it was done because they live in India. Probably, it could be better understood in the backdrop of the Hindutva advocates' commonly expressed view that 'India belongs to the Hindus. All other communities are part of Hinduism'.

Moreover, the past few decades have witnessed 'aggressive drive' to convert tribes to Hinduism by introducing caste system among the tribals (Roy 2013: 44). Similarly, the names of tribal people are being changed to Hindu names, and in quite few cases even Brahmins are being appointed in tribal villages which are a 'bit of scam' (Roy 2013: 45).

Subdivision of the Country into States

The construction of a particular political or cultural space necessarily involves simultaneous deconstruction of many spaces that do not fall in line with the reigning discourse of a country. Apart from many other facts of population, this point is also kept in view even in making the first-order political subdivision of a country. This happens because any administrative subdivision of a country into states and other spatial units is done with a view to create a specific politico-cultural space that goes in line with the political vision of the ruling class of the country. This is literally true of all countries, particularly the densely populated and old-settled ones, whether developed or developing.

Right after independence in 1947, India's political elite had opted for moving towards ethnic and cultural homogenization. Even Nehru was 'never very enthusiastic about linguistic provinces' (Das Gupta 1988: 188) particularly where majority of speakers were non-Hindus. No wonder, it is more than obvious that 'the map that emerged after Independence was, at least in part, an attempt to undermine or smother these 'traditional' identities and divides – including language/ethnic groups' (Mawdsley 2002: 128). For instance, the map of reorganized states of India in 1956 had no space for any of the tribal languages despite the fact that the tribal people together constitute a little above 8 per cent of the total population of the country, and in 14 per cent or 90 districts of the country their proportion was above 50 per cent even in 2011. Similarly, when the country was first reorganized into linguistic states in 1956, there were three large concentrations of tribal people in its middle part. Incidentally each of the three concentrations was bifurcated into four different linguistic states. This was done to marginalize not only their cultural, demographic and political identities but also the very possibility of their gaining political clout (Gill 2006: 101) in the heartland of India. Among other things, this has also made it easier to absorb them in Hinduism.

Why Religion-based Identity is Being Preferred?

The construction of a religion-based identity for political purposes is based on the assumption that there exists or should exist a uniform and homogeneous religious community for enabling better governance in the country. This assumption is certainly of doubtful nature since each religious community whether in India or in other countries often stands subdivided into quite many ethnic, social, linguistic or cultural groups. Generally speaking, larger the population of a religious community, the greater is the number of such subgroups.

Save a few small countries, each and every country is multi-ethnic, multicultural and multireligious. But the ruling elites of most of the countries like India design and conduct their politics and institutions in such a way that aims at homogenizing all differences within their territories.

This kind of effort is made because 'all that is challenging, singular, local – not to say all difference – appears threatening' and 'intrusive' to the ruling class Pandey (1992: 28), or to the very idea of homogenized national space. It is also true that such a comprehensive homogenization cannot be achieved until or unless some sort of foundational discourse is employed for constructing religious identities. If there is any opposition to such a discourse, then it is either ignored or ethicized, or is highlighted as an 'other' or even 'anti-national' that would stand marginalized in the national discourse, or might sometimes be subjected to degradation through collective violence or riots. Since such violence is viewed as 'exceptional and aberrant' (Pandey 1989: 28) in academic discourses, it soon loses its significance to any effective sociopolitical discourse or even to the cultural memory.

The main objective of promoting religion-based identity by the ruling class in Indian politics is to achieve homogenization not only within Hindus, the majority religious community, but also in the overall cultural space of the country. The achievement of this political objective involves both othering and deconstruction of smaller groups' identities. Consequently, besides cutting into the quality of democracy, it also degrades the relevance and significance of cultural heritage of different parts of the country, particularly that of smaller communities. Accordingly, this type of hegemony of 'a cultural or religious majority is seen as a direct threat' to the smaller groups (Bhambhri 2001: 192). For instance, such insecurity is bound to get furthered when minority communities see that 'Hindu cultural symbols are protected and promoted' and 'the minority cultural groups have been at the receiving end' (Bhambhri 2001: 179) particularly under the BJP-led governments. Thus, looking at some events in the country in recent decades, it appears that communalism and religious othering have become a 'part of the official doctrine' (Habib 2015: xxxv).

For the purpose of attaining its cherished goal of sociocultural homogenization, India's ruling class has adopted a 'highly centralized' discourse (Austin 1999: 1). Incidentally, such a centralizing political approach works to further sensitize various regional as well as ethnoreligious minority communities and encourage them to respond with politics based on their religious or ethnic identities and regional socio-economic problems. This sort of politics has continued in India since independence, and even before. The year 1967 was the beginning of coalition politics in many states the country. It is true that 'coalition is a region dictated political phenomenon. Despite being ideologically heterogeneous regional parties agree to come together on the basis of programmatic capability' (Chakrabarty 2008: 163). The elections in 1977, that came immediately after the end of the two years Emergency imposed by Indira Gandhi government, resulted in the huge defeat of the ruling Congress Party and the victory of Janata Party which was in fact a conglomerate of many political parties, including those operating at regional levels.

When religion-based identity is vigorously cultivated with some particular objective in mind, it certainly yields rich political dividends. For instance, the biggest ever electoral victory of the Congress party since independence was achieved in 1984 general elections that were held in the backdrop of the Blue Star Operation, the code name for the attack on the Golden Temple, the religious hub of the Sikh people, along with 37 other Sikh religious places in different urban centres, in June 1984; subsequently there came the widespread anti-Sikh violence for at least three to four days in Delhi and many other cities in North India in November 1984. Such a big victory for the congress, as it had won in 404 or 78.6 per cent of the parliamentary constituencies, did not happen even when it was expected to take place, that is, the first post-independence general election in 1952 when it registered victory in 74.4 per cent seats. It happened essentially for two, nay three reasons: (i) sympathy wave for Rajiv Gandhi and the party owing to the assassination of the former Prime Minister at the hands of her two security guards who were Sikhs; (ii) the fact that one small religious minority was strongly targeted with violence in the name of the unity and integrity of the country; and (iii) building up a highly negative stereotype of the Sikh community during 1983–1984. This election had taken place after 'the stupefying spectacle of officially sponsored communalism resulting in Operation Blue Star, the assassination and the holocaust of the Sikhs' (Kothari 1989: xxxiv). It was primarily the strong emotional and religious appeal of these factors, rather than any major achievement in socio-economic development, that had made all the difference for Congress party in this election.

Thus, there are several reasons behind the growing trend towards the use of religious identity in Indian politics. One, the compulsion of vote bank politics, that is, to bring people together for voting for a particular party or even parties in the name of religion. Not only it is easier to do it by appealing to religious emotions, the process of religion-based identity construction also attains its own momentum over a period of time. Second, if it is not done, then the elites of the scheduled and backward classes would come up with their own political parties as has already been the case for the past about three to four decades now. Three, since the large diversity of languages in India also give different as well as very effective options to organize people for politics, religion-based identity is often highlighted to keep people speaking different languages together; Four, different histories and distinct ethnic or religious experiences of some regions also furnish other paths of organizing people for politics. Last but not least, is the fact that being highly polylithic in nature, 'Hinduism had no centre' and the politicians 'want to provide a centre today' (Kothari 1989: 487).

The Role of Regional Identity

Interestingly, despite consistent efforts to build religion-based identities by various religious communities in the country, regional and ethnic identities have also got simultaneously sensitized. Significantly, the religious identity-based politics has also contributed a lot towards the rise of several new ethnic and regional identities. For instance, the demand for statehood by regionally concentrated ethnic groups in quite a few cases was to turn themselves into majority so that the region's language and other cultural symbols could be saved from degradation and possible extinction (Weiner 1997: 483). Actually, the political struggle now is not around one or two identities, but around several types of identities, that is, regional, religions, ethnic, language-based, cultural and past histories (Kumar 2011: 1). Similarly, there are caste- or caste-group-centric political parties. Besides, another 'limitation of ethno-religious mobilization is its reliance on emotions which often cover a number of different and contradictory motives' (Jeffrelot 1996: 528). Probably, the experience and memories of centuries of stigmatization and suppression of lower castes as well as backward castes on the part of 'upper' castes seems to have virtually made it very difficult for most of them to fully toe the political line suggested by the upper caste Hindu elites. But it is also true that if there happens to be a strong emotional irritant between Hindus and some other religious minority, then the weaker caste might get unified with upper caste Hindus in that area for some time at the most.

It has been rightly pointed out that 'India's historical evolution has been neither as a small-group-oriented culture nor a pan-Indian (classical, Islamic, and British-Indian) elite political culture, but rather both of these strands with an essential tension between them, and instead a dialectical transformation' (Singh 1990: 818). As pointed out earlier, India's large diversity – religious, ethnic, cultural and historical – has become so essential feature of the country's personality that adjusting this diversity in the political fabric of the country has become both a political challenge and a welcome opportunity to retain and celebrate it through symbiotic interaction. It needs to be kept in view that a country like India 'which is diverse on various counts, the idea of a single party or a leader or a single issue' that will inspire 'the country as a whole does not seem to be practical' (Chakrabarty 2008: 82).

The large diversity of the country is well manifested in the coalition governments both at the national level since 1989 and at state levels since 1967. For instance, it was after 30 years that a political party, BJP, had secured enough seats (282) in 2014 to be in a position to make national government at its own. It is another matter that it also opted for a coalition government, that is, National Democratic Alliance (NDA) government, with the help of its other alliance partners from regional parties. In other words, there has been always a coalition government at the national level since 1989. Even the Janata Party government that came to power in 1977 included quite a few regional parties in it. Therefore, it is not surprising that quite often 'regional/state level parties now negotiate with the dominant coalition making national party for crucial portfolios that allows to bring investments in their regions' (Kumar 2011: 2).

It is notable that, for one reason or another, it has been a period of coalition governments since 1989. In other words, the increasing importance of regional parties in Indian politics has led to, what Chakrabarty (2008: 12) rightly calls, 'regionalization of national politics' and 'nationalization of regional politics'. The results in favour of regional parties from the Bihar election in 2015, and from West Bengal, Tamil Nadu and Kerala elections in 2016, and these too in the backdrop of BJP wave in 2014, strongly reassert this position.

Both BJP and Indian National Congress (or Congress as it is commonly known) are the only two parties that have effective political as well as electoral visibility all over the country. All other parties – ideological, religious, regional and caste-based – are largely limited to one, two or, at the most, three states. Therefore, if the parliamentary seats won by both BJP and Congress are excluded, then the remaining seats could be singled out as belonging to the state-level regional parties or those having their effective spread over two to three states only. It becomes clear from Table 4.1 that the total number of seats held together by the two major parties – Congress and BJP – varied between 352 in 1991 and 282 in 1989. The rest of the seats were with the regional parties, religion-centric parties, caste-based parties, including those parties with effective electoral strength in two to three states only.

Table 4.1 *India: Parliamentary Seats Held by Congress Party and BJP, 1989–2014*

Election Year	*Congress*	*BJP*	*BJP + Congress*	*% of Total Seats*
1989	197	85	282	53.3
1991	232	120	352	67.6
1996	140	161	301	55.4
1998	101	182	283	52.1
1999	114	182	296	54.5
2004	145	138	283	52.1
2009	206	116	322	59.3
2014	44	282	326	60.0

Now the question arises as to why regional politics has been continually gaining strength despite the fact that religious identity has been increasingly employed in the Indian politics since 1947. This is because of the fact that 'Hindi sentiment and Hindu nationalism are ... as regionally based as linguistic-cultural attachments in the Indian union' (Brass 1974: 16). The same applies to most of the other languages from South India as well as those from East and Northeast India. Besides, it is also an important fact that the regional issues 'remain dominant in Indian society, in the economy, and in electoral politics' (Brass 1991: 156).

Summing Up

Religion-based identity provides an easy way to gaining and exercising political power as it is commonly considered a big help in building vote banks, even in the absence of good governance, essential for electoral politics in India. Most of the countries follow this strategy in politics, when one community, particularly that in majority, begins hard-binding its religious identity, then other communities also would necessarily follow suit. For the purpose of constructing religion-based identity and getting maximum political mileage out of it, the majority community would often take quite a few steps, such as (i) to put suitable provision in this regard in the Constitution of the country; (ii) to delineate administrative divisions of the country in such a way that subdivides degrades and marginalizes minority ethnic, linguistic and cultural groups to the maximum; (iii) to actively marginalize the discourses and sociocultural symbols of other religious, ethnic and regional communities so that such voices do not make clutter in the homogenizing agenda and (iv) to target one religious minority with covert or overt violence at a time in order to keep religious othering at the top that works to keep intact not only its vote bank, but also to keep together the huge diversity of the majority community. Strong religious othering becomes all the more necessary if the majority religious community itself has many ethnic divisions such as castes, capable of having their distinct discourses and vote banks. India's predominant political elites make use of all these inputs, whether directly or indirectly, in their struggle for political power.

It seems that the competition between religion-based identity politics aiming at highly centralized political system and the region-inspired coalition politics will continue for some time more until there happens a more constructive compatibility between centralizing and decentralizing views in the country's polity. This type of compatibility is a prerequisite for attaining healthy or symbiotic federal structure in the country. Although religion-based identity politics has been on the ascendency for a long time now, particularly since independence of the country, there are strong indications that the region-based identity politics would strongly forge ahead in near future. Besides, the requirements of good governance also call for that to happen. It can be safely said that 'coalition is perhaps the only political mechanism to provide stable government in India' (Chakrabarty 2008: 11) at both the national and the state levels. It becomes all the more essential when the idea of spatial or regional

democracy also becomes a part and parcel of the quest for better democratic framework.

References

Austin, Granville. 1999. *Working a Democratic Constitution: The Indian Experience Oxford*, Delhi: Oxford University Press.

Brass, Paul R. 1974. *Language, Religion and Politics in North India*, London: Cambridge University Press.

Brass, Paul R. 1991. *Ethnicity and Nationalism: Theory and Comparison*, Delhi: Sage Publications.

Bhambhri, C.P. 2001. *Bharatiya Janata Party: Periphery to Centre*, Delhi: Shipra Publications.

Chakrabarty, Bidyut. 2008. *Indian Politics and Society Since Independence: Events, Processes and Ideology*, London: Routledge.

Das Gupta, J. 1988. 'Ethnicity, Democracy and Development in India: Assam in a General Perspective', in *India's Democracy: An Analysis of Changing State-Society Relations*, A. Kohli (ed.), Princeton, NJ: Princeton University Press.

Ghurye, G.S. 1963. *The Scheduled Tribes*, Bombay: Popular Prakashan.

Gill, Mehar Singh. 2006. 'Situation of Tribal People in India', *Demography*, Published from Serbia, Vol. 3, pp. 91–104.

Habib, Irfan. 2015. 'Introduction', in *Religion in Indian History*, Irfan Habib (ed.), New Delhi: Tulika Books, for Aligarh Historians and Society, Fifth Edition, pp. xi–xli.

Jeffrelot, Christophe. 1996. *The Hindu Nationalist Movement in India*, New York: Columbia University Press.

Kothari, Rajni. 1989. *Politics and the People: In Search of a Humane India*, Delhi: Ajanta Publications.

Kumar, Ashutosh (ed.). 2011. 'Introduction', in *Rethinking State Politics of India: Religions within Religions*, London: Routledge.

Mawdsley, Emma. 2002. 'Regionalism, Decentralisation and Politics', in *South Asia in a Globalising World: A Reconstructed Regional Geography*, Glyn Williams and Robert W. Bradnock (eds.), Harlow, England: Pearson Education Limited, pp. 122–143.

Pandey, Gyanendra. 1992. 'In Defense of the Fragment: Writing about Hindu-Muslim Riots Today', *Representations*, No. 37, Special Issue: Imperial Fantasies and Postcolonial Histories, pp. 27–55.

Roy, Arundhati. 2013. *Broken Republic*, London, England: Penguin Books.

Singh, Mahendra Prasad. 1990. 'The Crisis of the Indian State: From Quiet Developmentalism to Noisy Democracy', *Asian Survey*, Vol. 30, No. 8, pp. 809–19.

Singh, Pritam. 2005. 'Hindu Bias in India's Secular Constitution: Probing Flaws in the Instrument of Governance', *Third World Quarterly*, Vol. 26, No. 6, pp. 909–26.

Weiner, Myron. 1997. 'Indian Minorities: Who Are They? What Do They Want?', in *State and Politics in India*, Chatterjee, Partha (ed.), Delhi: Oxford University Press.

5 Census and Colonialism

Tracing the Roots of Religious Demographic Anxiety

V. Sebastian

Since the inception of decennial census, numbers became an important element within the framework of religious identity in India. Basing on the 1891 census report, C.J. O'NDonnell (cited from C.F. Arnold, 1999: 137) pointed out the 'decline of Hinduism' and an increase of Mohammadans in Bengal during the past 20 years. He also pointed out that if this trend continued, with six centuries, Islam would become the universal religion of Bengal. Due to Malaria and famine, there had been large number of deaths especially in the Bengal presidency. Some of the Hindu intellectuals were anxious about these reports. One of the most influential tracts, namely, *Hindus: A Dying Race*, was produced in 1909 by U.N. Mukherji, who drew considerably from the census data to assess the Hindu decline. He attributed various reasons such as conversion, high death rate and a lack of vigour to the decline of Hindu population. Mukherji wrote: 'We are a dying race. Every census reveals the same face. We are getting proportionately fewer and fewer'. Having compared the Hindus to the 'dying races' such as the Maoris, Mukherji observed: 'The Mohammadans have a future and they believe in it – we Hindus have no conception of it. Time is with them – time is against us. At the end of the year they count their gains, we calculate our losses. They are growing in number, growing in strength, growing in wealth, growing in solidarity, we are crumbling to pieces. They look forward to a United Mohamaddan world – we are waiting for our extinction' (c.f. Arnold 1999: 137–38).

Closer to our own times, a book entitled *Religious Demography of India*, published by a right-wing group known as Center for Policy Studies (Chennai) in 2005 expresses similar fears about the 'Hindu decline.' L.K. Advani, the then Deputy Prime Minister, had written the Foreword for the same book which focuses on the 2001 census data. The assumptions about 'religions' made in this book are highly questionable to say the least. The authors *assume* that in ancient times, 'India' enjoyed cultural homogeneity which was destroyed by Islam and Christianity. These authors seem to take for granted that the ancient India had only one culture, namely, the *sanatana dharma*. Predictably, the consistent focus of this book is the 'quantum decline' of the 'Indian Religionists' and the corresponding increase of the Muslims and Christians – religions which have originated outside India. According to the same authors, the religious 'heterogeneity of the Indian population, and its division into mainly Hindus and Muslims, was a demographic reflection of relatively recent events in Indian history (Joshi, Srinivas and Bajaj 2005: 6–9).

The sudden release of the 2011 census data regarding religious demography on 25 August 2015 stands in the same continuum which reflects anxieties regarding the religious demography in India. While releasing the data, the Press Information Bureau (PIB) stated that the proportion of the Hindu population to the total population during the decade (2001--2011) had declined by 0.7 percentage point and that the proportion of the Muslim population to the total population had increased by 0.8 percentage point. The release of the data was followed by heated discussions about the religious demography in the media. Some of the Hindutva organizations responded with considerable alacrity. For example, the Vishwa Hindu Parishad leader Pravin Togadia demanded a peremptory imposition of the two-child norm among the Muslim community. Sakshi Maharaj, the BJP Lok Sabha member, who had a few months before exhorted Hindu women to produce four children each, demanded immediate steps to impose a uniform civil code and the two-child norm for Muslims. The Bihar unit of the Durga Vahini announced a house to house campaign in the state with a view of highlighting the 'perils pointed out by the Census 2011 data on religious communities'. Some analysts have pointed out the correlation between the timing of the release of the census data and the coming Bihar Assembly elections in October-November (Rajalakshmi and Ramakrishnan 2015: 5). What had been overlooked consists of the immense regional variations and nuances and the complexities involved in the interpretation of the census data.

All of these anxieties about religious demography have to do with the emergence of national space during colonial times and the contested nature of this national space in postcolonial era. These spatialized demographic fears reflect what Sankaran Krishna, a political theorist from the University of Hawaii, had termed as the 'cartographic anxiety'. Cartographic anxiety refers to the regional and nationalist anxiety about national identity and national space. Here, cartographic is understood not merely in terms of mapping, but rather the representational practices of space as well. For Krishna, the term 'cartography' means more than the scientific mapping of the country; it refers to the representational practices which attempts to inscribe something called India and the efforts to endow that entity with a content, history, trajectory and meaning. According to Krishna, cartographic anxiety is a dimension of the larger postcolonial anxiety syndrome exhibited by a society which sees itself as suspended forever in a space between the 'former colony' and 'not-yet-nation.' Post-colonial condition involves the efforts of colonial societies to catch up with the putative glorious pasts. In recent times, this cartographic anxiety has been represented and reflected in an overwhelming manner and in a variety of ways in India:

notions of security, purity, obsession with unity and the binary representational practices which define the Indian and the non-Indian, the patriot and the traitor, the insider and the outsider (Krishna 1994: 508). Perhaps one of the most controversial cartographic anxieties reflected in the right-wing ideology is the notion of 'Akhand Bharat, ('unified Bharat') a view held today by the RSS. The idea of a unified Hindu civilization exemplified in the Akhand Bharat dream includes not only Pakistan and Bangladesh, but also Afghanistan, Myanmar, Sri Lanka and Tibet. Most RSS literature pertaining to Akhand Bharat project it as a cultural entity rather than a political or a national one (Yadav 2016).

The recent focus of religious demography and Hindu nationalistic fervour reflect the same cartographic anxieties. I would like to suggest that the angst pertaining to religious demography has become an essential dimension of the cartographic anxieties. However, these cartographic anxieties have not come from thin air. I would like to suggest that the roots of these demographic and spatial anxieties have their origins in colonialism and their investigative modalities and administrative exigencies. In particular, the decennial census played a key role in the construction of religious communities of Hindus and Muslims which came to be seen as mutually exclusive. It has been pointed out time and again by scholars that census is not an apolitical matter and that the census had sharpened communal consciousness in both colonial and the post-colonial periods. It is argued in this chapter that the colonial administrative measure such as the census not only created categories which did not exist, but also made central aspect in the perception of identities. I will focus on two such categories, namely, 'religion' and 'Hindu' in this chapter.

In contemporary Indian sociopolitical and religious discourses, the term 'religion' and the term Hindu and its derivatives such as Hinduism, Hindustan and Hindutva have become highly charged terms, reflecting some of the unresolved tensions and significations inherited from the colonial past. Colonialism has a lot to do with some of these unsolved tensions and it becomes imperative to focus on the semantic horizon of these terms, especially that of 'religion' and that of 'Hinduism': How the term 'religion' came to acquire a commonsensical status in colonial India? What do the appellations Hindu and Hinduism signify? It is important to note that the 'notion of Hinduism' is itself a Western-inspired abstraction, which until the nineteenth century bore little or no resemblance to the diversity of Indian religious belief and practice' (King 1999b: 162). Ever since its introduction, the term 'Hinduism' in the sense of the 'religion of Hindus', various scholars have tried in vain to arrive at an acceptable definition of this religion (Stietencron 2001: 32). The orientalist construct was subsequently adopted by Hindu nationalists themselves in the quest for home rule (*swaraj*) and in response to British imperial hegemony (King 1999b: 156).

In the context of census, it must be remembered that the marker of identity called 'religion' did not exist in pre-colonial times in 'India'. It is with the British colonialism that the idea of 'religion' and Hinduism' as religion began to take shape. People of the Indian subcontinent did not have the notions of 'religion' and 'Hinduism' till the colonial scholars and administrators began to popularize it from the nineteenth century. It will be argued in this chapter that the categories of religion and Hinduism, which are made central in today's religious demography discourse by the right-wing groups, are artificial constructs introduced by the colonial administrators. In what follows, this chapter first locates the notion of 'religion' and how colonialism made it a central category in India. Secondly, it focuses on how colonial administrators made 'Hinduism' a monolithic entity and the role played by the decennial census.

The Concept of 'Religion'

As Richard King has pointed out, the term 'religion' clearly has a history that is bound up with the cultural and intellectual history of the West and deserves some attention. The key issue for King is this: The term 'religion' is a culturally specific social construction with a particular genealogy of its own. In applying this category to the study of non-Western cultures, one should be aware of the theological origins of the term. Further, one problem in discussions about the meaning, denotation and usefulness of the term 'religion' in a cross-cultural context is that the category itself is a privileged one (King 1999a: 156). This is especially true in the context of orientalist interpretation of Hinduism as a monolithic religion.

The term 'religion' derives from the Latin *religio*. In the pre-Christian era, Cicero provides an etymology of religion in terms of *relegere*, that is, to re-trace or re-read. Thus, religio denotes the retracing of 'the lore of the ritual' of one's ancestors. In the 'pagan' Roman Empire, this understanding of the term seems to have gained acceptance and the term *religio* was almost synonymous with *traditio*. Both these terms represented the teachings of one's ancestors which a particular tradition followed. From this perspective, for Romans, the newly arrived Christians were atheists since they did not accept the gods of Romans and the traditions of the state. The Romans saw Christianity as a superstition rather than a religion. As a new superstition, it could not claim the sanction of antiquity. Tacitus, who had nothing but contempt for the 'perverse and disgusting' customs of the Jews, admitted that 'Jewish worship is vindicated by its antiquity' (Benko 1984: 22). The legitimate religion in Rome was their own state cult or others which had been authorized. Foreign cults, including Judaism, were considered as superstition. As recent outgrowth of Judaism, Christianity could not claim the approval of antiquity and it shared the same disapproval of Judaism in the Roman Empire. Sect with foreign origin was *prava et externa religio* or a false and foreign religion (Benko 1984: 22). In the Roman Empire, public cults had been essentially a local and civic affair (Markus 1974: 28). Christians rejected all pagan cults and this caused much hatred and hostility in the empire. They also refused to take part in the emperor worship because of their monotheistic belief (Chadwick 1967: 27–8). Christian monotheism stood in sharp contrast to Roman *religio*. As a general policy, the Roman government was tolerant of existing cults provided the adherents of these cults did not encourage sedition and weaken the unity of the empire (Markus 1974: 15).

In the course of history, Christianity came to be seen not only as a religion but also as a religion *par excellence*. Justin Martyr (100–165) is one of the Christian Apologists defended Christianity against pagan criticism by arguing that traces of Christian truths were to be found in the ancient pagan writers. His doctrine *logos spermatikos* (seed-bearing word) affirmed that God had prepared the way for the final revelation in Christ in and through classical philosophy (McGrath 1994: 10–11). By co-opting pagan writers of antiquity, for Justin, Christian beliefs could gain some grounding in *traditio*. In the third century, we see with Lactantius (240–320), a Christian writer, a significant semantic shift of the term *religio*. Lactantius rejected Cicero's etymology and suggested that *religio* derives from re-ligare, meaning to bind together. For Lactantius, *religio* 'is the worship of the true; superstition of the false. And it is important, really why you worship, not how you worship, or what you pray for ... They are superstitious who worship many and false gods; but we, who supplicate the one true God, are religious' (c.f. Balagangadhara 1994: 62). With Christianity becoming the 'state' religion with the conversion of Constantine in AD 312, worshipping other gods were now seen as belonging to pagans (*paganus*: 'village idiot') and superstitious. 'The redefining of *religio* also served to establish the monotheistic exclusivism of Christianity as the normative paradigm for understanding what a religion is (King 1999a: 36–7).

Modern discussions of the meaning of the term 'religion' (*religio*) tend to follow Lactantius' etymology, thereby constructing a Christianized model of religion which strongly emphasizes theistic belief (monotheistic, polytheistic, henotheistic and pantheistic). According to King, even when Lactantius is not appealed to directly, 'religion' in a Christian (and post-Christian) context now becomes a matter of adherence to particular doctrines or beliefs rather than allegiance to ancient ritual practices (King 1999a: 37). As Robert Winthrop has pointed out, '[i]t is an inheritance of the Enlightenment, and less directly of the Reformation, to identify religion with the concept of belief, and hence with questions of truth and error. This modern sense is captured in the definition of religion given by the sociologist Emile Durkheim (1858–1917: 'a unified system of beliefs and practices relative to sacred things" (c.f. Winthrop 1991: 239).

In the early Christian context, the manner in which a number of heretical movements came to be seen as false doctrines and beliefs is an indicator to the extent truth and falsity (error) came to be seen as central in defining true religion (King 1999a: 39). Within such model, religion presupposes a literate tradition, in which specialists such as theologians who are responsible for codifying doctrine, regulating practice and rationalizing apparent inconsistencies (Winthrop 1991: 239). In the Western context, religion became primarily concerned with doctrines and true religion came to be seen as a matter of orthodoxy (King 1999a: 38). As far as the term 'religion' is concerned, such had been the Enlightenment legacy which the orientalists inherited and the term 'religion' has come to be seen as a universal category. As Balagangadhara has pointed out, Christianity has generally served as the prototypical example of a religion and thus as the fundamental yardstick or paradigm case for the study of other religions (Balagangadhara 1994: 307). Indeed, the numerous instances in which European writers, travellers and orientalists have described 'Hindu' beliefs and practices as superstitious and barbarous clearly presupposes an 'ideal' type of religion, which obviously, for most of them was Christianity.

As Balagangadhara (1994: 284–5) has pointed out, the largely uncontested status of the category 'religion' is reflected in the fact that in the West it is thought to be simply common sense that all cultures have religions and that those religions have been important constitutive factors in the development of those cultures. Difficulties and debates about the precise meaning of the term 'religion', and whether there is an 'essence' to religion, do not question the fundamental assumption that there are things called 'religions' that are easily identifiable and classified in terms of specific names such as Christianity, Islam, Hinduism, Buddhism, Jainism and Taoism.

In the colonial decennial census, the category called religion had already assumed considerable importance. 'Religion' came to be seen as a marker of difference between the West and the East. The West understood itself as rational and saw the Orient as 'religious', non-rational and superstitious. According to Gottschalk, religion always 'remained a marker of difference for Britons in their perception of South Asians' (2013: 51–2). At first it was the distinction between Christians, and India's Hindus and Muslims, but later between the more religious Indians and the more secular, rational Europeans. British Indologists held the view that because of the other-worldly orientation of the people of India, the key to understand the thinking of the Indian civilization lay in understanding its religious basis.

In the classificatory categories used in the census, in spite of ambiguities and complexities, 'religion' and 'caste' figured prominently. The question on religion was used by colonial administrators as a fundamental category in census tabulations and data on this published without any restraint (Bhagat 2001: 4352). The census data have been used historically 'not just for *enumeration* but also for *comparison*'. In the colonial as well as the postcolonial period, there is a near obsession to compare and contrast different religious communities (Gupta 2004: 4302). Hansen has noted how through the mediation of census the colonial government 'provided a new matrix of intelligibility through which the native subjects could come to know themselves as communities, and how this new matrix displaces older hierarchies and produced a social imaginary structured by consolidated – in principle equal – communities in competition' (2004: 36). It is not to be understood that the census gave castes new identities in simplistic terms; rather it means that the caste identities came to be seen in a new light of competition in terms of economic, social, cultural and political opportunities.

British taxonomy assumed both that communal and oppositional religious identities had existed since the rise of Muslim power in India in the twelfth century and that they represented the foundation of the Indian society and identity. However, precolonial indigenous classifications, by contrast, did not see religious identities as mutually exclusive. Available data would suggest that 'religious difference' was 'an inconsequential issue' (Gottschalk 2013: 105). But British colonialism brought about significant changes in the perception of religious identities. Through administrative measure and personal laws, colonialism did construct Hindu and Muslim identities as mutually exclusive. Directly and indirectly, the colonial administrators defined communities through mutually exclusive categories of social belonging that bifurcated nearly every societal and cultural dimension of India (Gottschalk 2013: 182–3). The decennial census was a key instrument which mediated the perception of identities because it classified all Indians by religion, which was the foundational category.

Hinduism as 'Religion'

Let us now focus on the idea of 'Hindu' and 'Hinduism' which the census enumerators take for granted as a monolith religious identity. Here our chief interest is the evolution of the term during the British colonial period. One of the earliest appellations for 'Hindu' employed by Europeans (including the early British orientalists) was 'Gentoo'. The term 'Gentoo' in these early European usages denote 'Gentile' or heathen. We find the term 'Gentile' applied to Indian population in the letters of Francis Xavier. In a letter written by Francis Xavier from Cochin to Father Simao Rodrigues in Portugal on 2 February 1549, he warns his friends in Europe that 'while they are ardently engaged in the pursuit of learning, they should not be so casual and unconcerned as to be completely indifferent to the ignorance and ruination of the Gentiles (Costelloe 1993: 243). Most of the early British orientalists used the terms 'Gentoo' and 'Hindoo' interchangeably. John Holwell (1711–1798), one of the early British orientalists, who lost rare manuscripts which he had collected 'with so much trouble and expenses', writes: 'It is well known that at the capture of Calcutta, AD 1756, I lost many curious manuscripts, and among them two very correct and valuable copies of the Gentoo *Shastah*' (Holwell 1767: 46). Holwell, who was a surgeon and worked for the East India Company, notes in the same writing that 'the perpetuity of the Gentoo doctrines, which through a succession of so many ages, have still remained unchanged, in their fundamental tenets ...' It needs to be noted here that Holwell does not use the term 'Gentoo' in any negative sense; in fact he very positive about the Gentoo beliefs which he tries to defend against those who have portrayed them in a negative light.

There is a tendency among the early orientalists to use both Gentoo and Hindoo. For instance, Nathaniel Halhed who translated and compiled *A Code of Gentoo Laws*, in which 'the genuine principles of the Gentoo jurisprudence are made public', notes in 'The Translator's Preface' that 'the Hindoos have no written laws whatever, but such as relate to the ceremonious peculiarities of their superstition' (Halhed 1776: 142). Halhed terms 'Brahmans' as 'the professors of the ordinances', and ordinary people 'pay them besides a degree of personal respect little short of idolatry' (1776: 142). Halhed suggests that 'Hindostan' is a Persian and foreign appellation, and that 'Hindostan is constantly denominated Bhertekhunt or Jumbudweep' and concludes with the observation: 'Hindoo therefore is not the term by which the inhabitants originally stiled themselves, but according to the idiom of their language, Jumbudweepee or Bhertekhunte; and it is only since the era of the Tartar government that they have assumed the name of Hindoos, to distinguish themselves from their conquerors, the Mussulmen' (Halhed 1776: 150). More than other orientalists of his time, Halhed seems to be aware of the nuances inherent in the appellations of Hindoo and Gentoo and he suggests that the notion of Gentoo, as used by Europeans to cover the whole of Hindus, is a mistaken one:

> The word Gentoo has been, and is still, equally mistaken to signify, in the proper sense of the term, the professors of the Brahminical religion, whereas Gent, or Gentoo, means animal in general, and in its more confined sense, mankind; but is never, in the Sanskrit dialect, nor even in the modern jargon of Bengal, appropriated particularly to such as follow the doctrines of Brahma. The four great tribes have each their own separate appellation; but they have no common or collective term that comprehends the whole nation under the idea affixed by Europeans to the word Gentoo (Halhed 1776: 150).

When Europeans began to use the term 'Hindoo', they applied it to the non-Muslim population of India without scholarly differentiations (Stietencron 2001: 33). As Frykenberg has pointed out, in the eighteenth century references to 'Hindoo' Christians and 'Hindoo' Muslims were not uncommon: 'Thus, as already indicated, during the late eighteenth century when the concept first began to be used, the term 'Hindu' was applied to anything which was of India, anything 'Native,' or 'Indian''. As such, as a sociopolitical concept, it related especially to things pertaining to the cultures and peoples of Hinduism proper, or even to the same in South India. In this sense, references to 'Hindoo' Christians or 'Hindoo' Muslims, namely, references to Christians and Muslims, of India who were characteristically and distinctively 'Hindoo' or Indian in their culture and style of life are not uncommon' (Frykenberg 2001: 85).

The concept of 'Hindu' was also used as a term of exclusion: 'It was the term used, in negative ways, to characterize all things in India (especially elements and features found in the cultures and religions of India) which were not Muslim, not Christian, not Jewish or, hence, not Western. 'Hindu', in this sense, was term of 'exclusion' (Frykenberg 2001: 85). The Hindus were defined as, 'a native of India who is not of European, Armenian, Moghul, Persian or other foreign descent, who is a member of a recognised caste, who acknowledges the spiritual authority of brahmans, who venerates or at least refuses to kill or harm kine, and does not profess any creed or religion which the brahman forbids him to profess' (Bhagat 2001: 4354). Interestingly, such negative contrast is present in the modern Indian law. For instance, the 1955 Hindu Marriage Act, Section 2 (1), defines a 'Hindu' as a category which includes not only all Buddhists, Jains and Sikhs but also anyone who is not a Muslim, a Christian, a Parsee or a Jew (King 1999b: 163). P.J. Marshall describes the hermeneutic horizon within which orientalists understood and interpreted 'Hinduism':

> English writers in the second half of the eighteenth century were the heirs to over 200 years of attempts by Europeans to interpret Hinduism. Interpretations had generally followed the same lines: comparatively soon Europeans had begun to make the distinction, which was to have so long a life, between what they regarded as 'popular' Hinduism and 'philosophical' Hinduism. Popular cults were described to be condemned or ridiculed, but most writers were also prepared to admit the existence of metaphysical assumptions and ethical doctrines in Hinduism of which they could approve because they seemed to be similar to Western concepts, although the similarities which they found now seem to depend largely on the inability of Europeans to describe a religious system except in Christian terms (Marshall 1970: 20).

The chief focus of the early orientalists in interpreting Hinduism had been Sanskrit texts. It is important for our purpose to take into cognizance the fact that the orientalist interpretation of Hinduism as a monolithic 'religion' like Semitic religions did influence Indian nationalists, majority of whom came from the classical traditions of India. Romila Thapar describes the Semitic or Judeo-Christian framework within which the orientalists interpreted 'Hindu' religious tradition and its effect in the following manner:

> The Orientalist attempt at integrating religious belief and practice into a coherent religion and a rational faith known as Hinduism, was from the perspective of Semitic religions since these were more familiar to such scholarship. These views had an influence to a greater or lesser extent on the socio-religious reform movements of the nineteenth and early twentieth centuries. Many of the projections of the Hindu religion today are also derived from treating it as parallel to some vaguely understood Semitic form. This is rather different from what the indigenous sources suggest. (Thapar 1991: 21)

The indigenous sources never used an all-embracing term which was intended to cover various belief systems and practices of 'Hindus'. According to Joseph T. O'Connell, the word 'Hindu' appeared in *Gaudiya Vaisnava* texts of the sixteenth century (c.f. Frykenberg 2001: 84). But here the term 'Hindu' appears only in texts describing incidents of strained relationship between Hindus as natives and Muslims as foreigners ('Yavanas' or 'Mlecchaas'). The term was never used by Hindus among themselves to describe themselves; moreover, the term 'Hindu dharma', which occurs seven times, was only used in the same way and never with any explicit definition or discussion of what 'Hindu' or 'Hindu dharma' itself meant. Frykenberg concludes that 'Hindu dharma', therefore, is the closet resemblance to the term 'Hinduism' which can be found to have arisen out of indigenous sources within India' (Frykenberg 2001: 84). However, it needs to be noted that the term 'Hindu dharma' of indigenous sources may not correspond to the modern designation of 'Hinduism' as an all-embracing and monolithic entity which it eventually came to represent in the nineteenth century.

The attempts to create a monolithic, and uniform religion, which Romila Thapar terms as 'syndicated Hinduism', which is a fundamental departure from the essentials of what may be called the indigenous 'Hindu' religions. According to Thapar, a reference to 'Hinduism' would require a more precise definition and needs to be concretized in terms of diverse and distinct traditions such as Brahmanism, Tantrism, Shaivism, Vaishnavism, Shaktism, numerous *sampradaya* and countless concrete manifestations of popular religiosity such as folk Hinduism (Thapar 2001: 54–81). According to Thapar, bunching together these diverse religious phenomena under the monolithic heading of Hinduism violates particular and historical traditions. Much of the distinctions within these diverse traditions also need to be located within the purity–impurity practices. For instance, a vast majority of the so-called dalits and untouchables who adhere to folk Hinduism have their rituals conducted by non-Brahmin priests. Brahmin priests cannot perform many of the rituals of folk Hinduism as these rituals involve alcohol and meat which are considered impure by the mainstream Hinduism (Thapar 2001: 54–81).

Indeed, the bewildering diversity of beliefs and practices of the Indian subcontinent did not easily fit into the standard notion of 'religion' held by early Indologists. David Kopf, who has uncritical appreciation for the British orientalists, describes their efforts in homogenizing 'Hinduism' into a coherent religion: 'The work of integrating a vast collection of myths, beliefs, rituals and laws into a coherent religion, and of shaping an amorphous heritage into a rational faith known now as 'Hinduism' were endeavours initiated by Orientalists' (c.f. King 1999b: 165). Eventually, both British orientalists and imperialist historians began to interpret 'Hinduism' as a monolithic entity. Such essentialized discursive practices are reflected in the works of Vincent Smith, one of the imperialist historians: 'If all references to Islam, Christianity and other foreign religions be put aside for a moment, it may be said that India, excepting uncultured tribes, is essentially Hindu, the land of the Brahmans. The unity underlying the obvious diversity of India may be summed up in the word Hinduism' (Smith 1958: 26).

As we noted, one of the new ideas introduced by the colonial administrators was the notion of 'religion'. But not every Indian agreed with such novel ideas. Bankim Chandra Chatterjee, a famous Bengali novelist of the nineteenth century, writes about the mistaken notion of *dharma* as Hindu religion:

> Search through all the vast literature of India, and you will not, except in modern writings where Hindu has sought obsequiously to translate the phraseology of his conquerors, meet with any mention of such a thing as the *Hindu religion*. Search through all the vast records of pre-Mohamedan India, nowhere will you meet with even such a word as *Hindu*, let alone Hindu religion. Nay more. Search through the whole of that record, and nowhere will you meet with such a word as *religion*. The word *Dharma*, which is used in the modern vernaculars as its equivalent, was never used in pre-Mohamedan India in the same sense as Religion ... For religion [the pre-Mohamedan Hindu] had no name, because he never entertained any conception to which such a name would have been applicable. (c.f. Lariviere 1989: 758)

As we have seen, the term 'Hindu' is not a self-designation of the 'Hindus' and the term 'Hindu' began to be used by the 'Hindus' only in the sixteenth century. However, it needs to be noted that the term 'Hindu dharma' of indigenous sources may not correspond to the modern designation of 'Hinduism' as an all-embracing and monolithic entity, which it eventually came to represent in the nineteenth century. The colonial administrative exigencies, especially the decennial census, contributed to the reinforcement of 'Hinduism' as a monolithic entity. It is not suggested here that the decennial census is the key contributor to such Hindu identity constructions. There are other colonial administrative measures such as the Hindu Personal Law which had made its contribution to the construction of a unified Hindu identity.

Conclusion

There are very few things in the post-independent India which have gained permanence as religion as the marker of identity. The unstated assumption in the right-wing ideologies makes one thing clear: the priority of Hindus over other groups rest on the numerical aspect, namely, the Hindus form the majority religion in India. The notion of 'majority' and 'minority' began to circulate in the official and political domain in colonial times. This idea was brought into the political consciousness with the beginning of decennial census which began in 1871 by colonial administrators. As B. Cohn has pointed out, the 'census was one of the situations in which Indians were confronted with the question of who they were and what their social and cultural systems were' (2004: 248). One of the inadvertent results of the decennial census was the induction of the new notion of 'majority' and 'minority' communities. According to Dirks, 'one of the major consequences of the census was the denomination of 'Hindus' as the majority group in India, with 'Muslims' as the dominant minority, atop groups of other, progressively smaller, discrete religious communities' (Dirks 2003: 255). Recently, Amartya Sen has pointed out that the very classificatory scheme such as 'majority' and 'minority', which has been accepted as common sense, itself is problematic. Sen writes:

> What is seen as a majority depends critically on what principle of classification is used. The people of India can be classified on the basis of different criteria, of which religion is only one. It is, for example, also possible to categorize Indians according to class, or language, or literature or political beliefs, to mention just a few. (Sen 2005: 55)

Amartya Sen writes further: In order to attach immense significance to the fact that Hindus constitute a majority group in Indian society in one particular system of classification, the priority of that religion-based categorization over other systems of classification would have to be established first' (Sen 2005: 55).

Does religion needs to be a central aspect of our identity? There has been a tendency from colonial times, especially after the census enumerations began, to project the category of 'religion' as a key classificatory category. The orientalist constructions, especially of the Romantic type, projected India as fundamentally religious. This orientalist construction had been put to use in the nationalist discourse which saw India as far superior in religiosity, spirituality and in philosophy to the West. Thus, Vivekananda wrote: 'To the other nations of the world, religion is one among the many occupations of life ... But here, in India, religion is the one and the only occupation of life' (1993a: 2–3). Vivekananda wrote time and again that India is fundamentally a religious country: 'The Indian mind is first religious, then anything else' (1993b: 74–5). According to Vivekananda:

> the one common ground that we have is our sacred tradition, our religion. That is the only common ground, and upon that we shall have to build. In Europe, political ideas form the national unity. In Asia, religious ideals form the national unity. The unity of religion, therefore, is absolutely necessary as the first condition of the future of India. (1993b: 70)

Is there any basis for such assertions by Indian nationalists and spiritual gurus? Someone familiar with colonial history would recognize the fact that the orientalists such as Max Müller had played a big role in the creation of such myths. Those who are familiar with history would recognize that such myths came very useful for the Indian nationalists in their quest to create a pan-Indian identity. We need to ask further: Does such interpretation stand on reasonable grounds? According to Romila Thapar, a well-known historian:

> Indians in the pre-eighteenth century never claimed that they were more spiritual than other peoples, or that the Indian way of life was concerned solely with things spiritual. The ideal of the earlier texts that the best life on earth is a balance between dharma, artha, and kama, shows a healthy unconcern for any obsession with either the spiritual or the material. (1979: 7)

Many countries in the world do not include the question of religion in their census. For example, the official United States census does not ask one's religious affiliation (Merriman 2009: 11). However it is not often remembered that the very taxonomy of 'religion' in India is a colonial invention, which had been reinforced time and again through the decennial census. Though belonging to the category of what historian Eric Hobsbawm has termed as the 'invented tradition', the taxonomy of 'religion' has gained the status, both as an objective reality and as identity marker over the years. Most social scientists, the media and the 'religious' fundamentalists tend to take the taxonomy of religion as a 'given' fact. Unfortunately in India there are hardly any serious debates taking place in the public sphere and in the academia regarding the colonial legacies and heritages which we still carry on.

References

Arnold, David. 1999. 'An Ancient Race Outworn: Malaria and Race in Colonial India, 1860–1930', in *Race, Science and Medicine, 1700–1960*, Bernard Harris and Waltraud Ernst (eds.), London: Routledge, pp. 123–43.

Balagangadhara, S.N. 1994. *The Heathen in His Blindness: Asia, the West, and the Dynamic of Religion*, Leiden: E.J. Brill.

Benko, Stephen. 1984. *Pagan Rome and the Early Christians*, London: B.T. Batsford Ltd.

Bhagat, R.B. 2001. 'Census and the Construction of Communalism in India', *Economic and Political Weekly*, Vol. XXXVI, Nos. 46–47, 24 November, pp. 4352–6.

Chadwick, Henry. 1967. *The Early Church*, Middlesex: Penguin Books.

Cohn, Bernard. 2004. 'The Census, Social Structure and Objectification in South Asia', in *An Anthropologist among the Historians and Other Essays*, New Delhi: Oxford University Press, pp. 224–54.

Costelloe, Joseph (tr. and ed.). 1993. *The Letters and Instructions of Francis Xavier*, Anand: Gujarat Sahitya Prakash.

Dirks, Nicholas. 2003. *Castes of Mind: Colonialism and the Making of Modern India*, Delhi: Permanent Black.

Frykenberg, Robert Eric. 2001. 'The Emergence of Modern 'Hinduism' as a Concept and as an Institution: A Reappraisal with Special Reference to South India', in Günther-Dietz Sontheimer and Hermann Kulke (eds.), *Hinduism Reconsidered*, New Delhi: Manohar Publications, pp. 82–107.

Gottschalk, Peter. 2013. *Religion, Science and Empire: Classifying Hinduism & Islam in British India*, New York: Oxford University Press.

Gupta, Charu. 2004. 'Censuses, Communalism, Gender and Identity', *Economic and Political Weekly*, Vol. XXXIX, No. 39, 25 September, pp. 4302–4.

Halhed, Nathaniel Brassey. 1776. 'The Translator's Preface to a Code of Gentoo Laws', *The British Discovery of Hinduism in the Eighteenth Century* [published in 1776], in P.J. Marshall (1970), Cambridge: Cambridge University Press, pp. 140–91.

Hansen, Thomas Blom. 2004. *The Saffron Wave: Democracy and Hindu Nationalism in Modern India*, Princeton University Press, 1999. Reprint, 2004, New Delhi: Oxford University Press.

Holwell, John Zephaniah. 1767. 'The Religious Tenets of the Gentoos', *The British Discovery of Hinduism in the Eighteenth Century* (first published in 1767), Reprint, P.J. Marshall, (1970), Cambridge: Cambridge University Press.

Joshi, A.P., M.D. Srinivas and J.K. Bajaj. 2005. *Religious Demography of India*, Chennai: Centre for Policy Studies.

King, Richard. 1999a. *Orientalism and Religion: Postcolonial Theory, India and 'The Mystic East'*, New Delhi: Oxford University Press.

King, Richard. 1999b. 'Orientalism and the Modern Myth of Hinduism', *Numen*, Vol. 46, No. 2, pp. 146–85.

Krishna, Sankaran. 1994. 'Cartographic Anxiety: Mapping the Body Politic in India', *Alternatives*, Vol. 19, pp. 507–21.

Lariviere, Richard. 1989. 'Justice and *Panditas*: Some Ironies in Contemporary Readings of the Hindu Legal Past', *The Journal of Asian Studies*, Vol. 48, No. 4, November, pp. 757–69.

Marshall, P.J. 1970. *The British Discovery of Hinduism in the Eighteenth Century*, Cambridge: Cambridge University Press.

Markus, R.A. 1974. *Christianity in the Roman World*, London: Thames and Hudson.

McGrath, Alister. 1994. *Christian Theology: An Introduction*, Oxford: Blackwell.

Merriman, Scott. 2009. *Religion and the State: An International Analysis of Roles and Relationships*, California: ABC Clio.

Rajalakshmi, T.K. and Venkitesh Ramakrishnan. 2015. 'Population Politics', *Frontline*, Vol. 32, No. 19, 2 October, pp. 4–14.

Sen, Amartya. 2005. 'India: Large and Small', in *The Argumentative Indian: Writings on Indian Culture, History and Identity*, London: Penguin Books, pp. 45–72.

Smith, Vincent. 1958. *Oxford History of India*, Oxford: Oxford University Press, 1919, Third edition.

Stietencron, Heinrich von. 2001. 'Hinduism: On the Proper Use of a Deceptive Term', in Günther-Dietz Sontheimer and Herman Kulke (eds.), *Hinduism Reconsidered,* Delhi: Manohar Publications, pp. 32–53.

Thapar, Romila. 1979. *The Past and Prejudice*, New Delhi: National Book Trust.

Thapar, Romila. 1991. 'Communalism and Historical Legacy: Some Facets', in K.N. Panikkar (ed.), *Communalism in India: History, Politics and Culture*, New Delhi: Manohar Publications, pp. 17–33.

Thapar, Romila. 2001. 'Syndicated Hinduism', in Günther-Dietz Sontheimer and Hermann Kulke (eds.), *Hinduism Reconsidered*, New Delhi: Manohar Publications, pp. 54–81.

Vivekananda. 1993a. 'India's Message to the World', in *My India, Arise,* Calcutta: Ramakrishna Math and Ramakrishna Mission, pp. 1–6.

Vivekananda. 1993b. 'The Future of India', in *My India, Arise,* Calcutta: Ramakrishna Math and Ramakrishna Mission, pp. 68–94.

Winthrop, Robert. 1991. *Dictionary of Concepts in Cultural Anthropology,* New York: Greenwood Press.

Yadav, Shyamlal. 2016. 'RSS & Akhand Bharat', *The Indian Express*, 5 January.

6 Demography, Minorities and Communalism

Ambrose Pinto

As long as demography studies both quantitative and qualitative aspects of human population, in India it is often used by vested interest group to serve their larger designs. There are no major issues when one examines the quantitative aspects of demography such as composition, density, distribution, growth, movement, size and structure of the population. It is the qualitative aspects such as caste, religion, growth of communities, quality of education, crime, development, diet and nutrition, social class, wealth and well-being that are made use of by communalists to further their ends. The increase or decrease of population of minority communities is interpreted by the communalists to suit their long-term interests. The Hindutvavadis had stated in several pronouncements that the minorities are increasing their numbers by conversions, love jihad and through reproductive process and that they are heading for minority status. These elements had proposed anti-conversion laws, *'Ghar Wapsi'* programmes and action against 'love jihad'. They have alleged that Muslim households multiply faster than the majority community households. The Christians are said to be increasing due to conversions. Fear is created in the minds of the citizens that one day the minorities would take over the country if they multiply in the manner they do and if conversions go on. Population growth rates, when disaggregated along religious lines, provide fodder for religious extremists, who use the figures to fan communalism. Howard Wriggins and James Guyot have noted that demographic changes can cause competing ethnic elites to worry that their groups' reduced numbers would cost them political clout and thereby 'precipitate ethnic group conflict' (1973: 6).

Census 2011

This chapter will look at the census data 2011 of the two main religious communities of India, Muslims and Christians versus the Hindu population released by the Government of India on 25 August 2011 and make a case how the Hindutva groups and a section of the media have used these data to sensationalize and create controversies. The consistent theme in most created controversies is that the Hindu population is on the decline and the Muslim and Christian population is on the increase. The increase, in the perception of the communalists of the Muslim population, is because Muslim men are allowed to marry more than one wife and in the case of Christian population it is due to conversion. To the communalists even if the objective figures do not prove the premise, they have been in a position to interpret the figures in terms of their larger game.

Table 6.1 *Population Growth for Hindus and Muslims during 2001 to 2011*

	All India	*Hindu*	*Muslim*
Population in 2001	1.02 billion	827 million	138 million
Population in 2011	1.21 billion	966 million	172 million
Population Growth	181 million	138 million	34 million
Share of population – 2001	100	80.46	13.43
Share of population – 2011	100	79.80	14.23
Growth Rate (2001–2011)	100	16.80	14.23

Source: Census 2011 data on Population by Religious Communities, Government of India.

Table 6.2 *Population Trends for Major Religious Groups in India (1951–2011)*

Religious group	*Population % 1951*	*Population % 1961*	*Population % 1971*	*Population % 1981*	*Population % 1991*	*Population % 2001*	*Population % 2011*
Hinduism	84.1	83.45	82.73	82.30	81.53	80.46	79.8
Islam	9.8	10.69	11.21	11.75	12.61	13.43	14.2
Christianity	2.3	2.44	2.60	2.44	2.32	2.34	2.3
Sikhism	1.79	1.79	1.89	1.92	1.94	1.87	1.7
Buddhism	0.74	0.74	0.70	0.70	0.77	0.77	0.7
Jainism	0.46	0.46	0.48	0.47	0.40	0.41	0.4
Zoroastrianism	0.13	0.09	0.09	0.09	0.08	0.06	n/a
Ethnic faiths, others	0.43	0.43	0.41	0.42	0.44	0.72	n/a

Source: Census of India.

The figures in Table 6.1 show that in the last decade while the percentage of Hindu population has declined, the Muslim population has increased and the Christian population has remained constant. In terms of numbers, all communities have grown. The Hindu population has increased by 138 million. This numerical growth is roughly equivalent of the entire Muslim population of 2001. On the other hand, the growth rate for Muslims is declining and the decline is higher than the Hindu community. Rate of decline over the decade for Muslim population (4.9%) is marginally higher than for Hindu population (3.5%). The sex ratio for Hindu community has improved marginally and it has significantly improved for the Muslim community.

Response of the RSS

Soon after the census report were out in the media, the RSS had suggested that the Hindus should revisit their practice of 'blindly accepting' family planning methods and start embracing big family norms. This would help check the reported demographic shift that is happening in favour of minorities in certain parts of the country, RSS joint secretary Dattatreya Hosabale had told reporters (Ramavarman 2013). He had said the 2011 census figures had indicated that the growth rate of children in the 0–6 age group was 15 per cent among Hindus and 18 per cent among Muslims. He suggested that each family should have at least three children. Hosabale claimed that former RSS leader late K.S. Sudarshan had also suggested that Hindu families should have more children. 'We don't have adequate number of youths to join our armed forces. The one-child family prefers their children to join sectors like IT' (Ramavarman 2013). Behind the statements is a message that religion matters and any decline in the Hindu population and increase in Muslim population is going to have consequences for the country.

The Hindutva Narrative on Population Growth of Minorities

The BJP and its allies continue their effort to shape the narrative around the growth of India's Muslim and Christian

Table 6.3 *Religion-wise Growth and Work Participation (Rural and Urban)*

Religious group	Population %	Growth (1991–2001)	Sex ratio (total)	Literacy (%)	Work participation (%)	Sex ratio (rural)	Sex ratio (urban)	Sex ratio (child)
Hinduism	80.46	20.3	931	65.1	40.4	944	894	925
Islam	13.43	29.3	936	59.1	31.3	953	907	950
Christianity	2.34	22.6	1,009	80.3	39.7	1,001	1,026	964
Sikhism	1.87	18.2	893	69.4	37.7	895	886	786
Buddhism	0.77	18.2	953	72.7	40.6	958	944	942
Ethnic faiths, others	0.72	103.1	992	47.0	48.4	995	966	976
Jainism	0.41	26.0	940	94.1	32.9	937	941	870

population. As per the census 2011 (Table 6.2), Muslims are now 14.2 per cent of the total population (a rise of 0.8% in the last decade), while Hindus have dropped below the 80 per cent mark to 79.8 per cent of the total population (a fall of 0.7%). It is also correct that the rate of growth among Muslims has been 24.6 per cent, and the same has been 16.8 per cent among Hindus. However, the above data do not tell us the full truth. The 2011 census data tell us that there is a declining trend in the growth rate of Muslims over the last three decades, and that it is sharper than the Hindu community. In fact, the rate of growth among the Muslim population has been falling consistently over the last three decades from 34.5 per cent in 1991 to 29.5 per cent in 2001, and now 24.6 per cent in 2011 census. In terms of absolute numbers, there are now 2.4 crores more Muslims since the last decade, and 13.9 crore more Hindus. Hence, the 2011 census data counter claim that Muslims will soon overtake Hindus in India. Besides, higher growth rate does not have to be attributed only to increase in birth rate. Any community or group with less number of women, even if the birth rate is the same, will have lesser proportion in total population. Census 2011 tells us that the number of women per thousand men among Muslims is 951, and while among Hindus it is only 939. The data indicate the practice of foeticide in both the communities, though lesser in Muslim communities. Foeticide resulting in decline of sex ratio may affect the proportion of population of one community or group even if the birth rate is the same.

However, one is not surprised at the outbursts and interpretation of the increasing population of the Muslim community by the Sangh Parivar. Being anti-minority, every hard data have to be interpreted to suit their long-term agenda. What surprised many is the attack on the Christian community in spite of the population remaining stable by Surjit Bhalla (http://indianexpress.com), contributing editor, *The Indian Express*, and senior India analyst, the Observatory Group, a New York-based policy advisory group in two of his articles that appeared on the 1 and 5 September 2015 in *The*

Indian Express. Being committed to an ideology, he is a representative of that ideology. The question that he raised was, in spite of having highest level of female education and the lowest fertility rate, why is the Christian population growth rate the same as that of the average Indian? What Bhalla wants to prove is that the conversion issue is not an issue of propaganda but it is real and it exists. He argues that 'along with Sikhs, Christians are the richest community in India (which is highly debatable. Christians surely are not the second richest community in India). In the early 1990s, mean per capita consumption of Christians was ₹ 404 per month and the fertility rate was 3.8 children per woman. The corresponding numbers for Sikhs was ₹ 473 and 3.9'. It was almost identical:

If so, then the population growth rate of Christians should be virtually identical to that of Sikhs; actually, somewhat less because of the higher education level and slightly lower fertility rate. But that is manifestly not so. Between 1991 and 2011, the Sikh population grew at an average rate of 1.2 per cent per annum, while the population growth rate of Christians was a relatively higher 1.9 per cent per annum. This growth rate was higher than that of Hindus (1.8 per cent) and almost exactly equal to the average for all religions. So, despite having the highest per capita consumption, the highest level of female education and the lowest fertility, the Christian growth rate is the same as that of the average Indian. (http://indianexpress.com)

His conclusion therefore was in accordance with his thesis that Christianity practices proselytization:

> If Christians had the same population growth rate as Sikhs (of 1.2 per cent a year rather than the actual growth rate of 1.9 per cent a year), the total number of Christians in India would have been 24.1 million. The 'excess' Christian population of 3.7 million in 2011 is very likely due to conversions. This excess translates into an average conversion rate of 1.7 lakh per year between 1991 and 2011.

The other allegation that he makes of the community is of receiving foreign funds, another stereotype. Quoting from the annual report of the Ministry of Home Affairs' annual report 2011–2012, he says, Christian missionary organizations, collectively received ₹ 2,003.75 crore as foreign contributions:

> In that year, a total of ₹ 11,000 crore was received by all NGOs. Assuming this money was mostly for conversions, a lower bound estimate of conversion expenditures can be obtained: approximately ₹ 1.1 lakh per person or ₹ 5.5 lakh for a family of five (again, assuming that a family is converted together). The actual conversion expenditures are possibly lower; equally, possibly higher. However, it is quite unlikely that a poor converted family gets an amount in the range of several lakhs – if so, newspapers would have reported it! Since souls are being saved by the modern evangelicals, one presumes they don't charge a fat salary to convert poor, desperate Hindus. But apparently they do. (http://indianexpress.com)

There could not have been a worse argument than what is presented of establishing a connection between funds received from NGOs and the money used for conversions.

In an article on 1 September 2015 'Bend It Like Bhalla', Tony Joseph (http://indianexpress.com), a former editor of *Business World* magazine, responded to Bhalla stating that 'On census, Christians and Conversions', Surjit Bhalla has tortured his data to make it say what he wants to hear. 'The device that Bhalla uses to make his argument is a comparison between the behaviour of the Christian and Sikh populations. According to him, the education levels of Sikh and Christian women are comparable, and because women's literacy is one important determinant of fertility rates, he argues that Christian and Sikh populations should behave similarly. And since, according to the census figures, the Sikh population declined from 2 per cent of the total in 1991 to 1.7 per cent in 2011, while the Christian population percentage stayed stable, he asserts that the difference can only be attributed to conversions. This amounts to serial assaults on data', says Tony Joseph. According to him, Bhalla has arbitrarily chosen the years to fit his theory. If one takes 1971 as the starting point, instead of 1991, as Bhalla has

done, one will find that the Christian population has declined from 2.6 to less than 2.3 per cent, a decrease of over 0.3 percentage points in 40 years. During the same period, the Sikh population declined from 1.9 to 1.7 per cent, a decline of only 0.2 percentage points. So which community declined more in population-percentage terms depends entirely on the period one chooses. That Bhalla chose the period he did shows us what result he wanted to arrive at. The second response Tony Joseph makes to Bhalla's allegations is that 'he omits mentioning a crucial factor of the difference in the sex ratio between the two communities he has chosen to compare. In communities that have a strong preference for sons and adopt practices such as sex selection, the sex ratio becomes highly skewed against women. Among Christians, there are 1,023 females for every 1,000 males, while among Sikhs, there are only 903 females for every 1,000 males. It is a well-known and academically accepted fact that highly skewed sex ratios like this have a significant impact on population growth'. Among the many reasons for the decline of the population, and among them, the major cause is the lowest sex ratio among Sikhs at the national level. In other words, Sikh population growth is likely to be abnormally depressed because of the adverse sex ratio, a problem that the Christian community does not have. So the kind of Christian–Sikh comparison that Bhalla makes is prima facie indefensible. Again, the fact that he found it necessary to omit any mention of the vast difference in sex ratio between the two communities only shows us what result he wanted. Thirdly, Tony Joseph said that Bhalla chose to compare the Christian community with Sikhs, and not with Jains, who are leagues above both Christians and Sikhs when it comes to women's literacy and income levels. Jain women have a literacy rate that is over 90 per cent, compared to only about 76 per cent for Christians and 63 for Sikhs. According to Bhalla's theory, therefore, the population percentage of Jains should have fallen drastically, even more so than that of Sikhs. But what do we find? In the 20 years between 1991 and 2011, the period that Bhalla considers, the proportion of Jains in the population has remained rock steady at 0.4 per cent. The fact that Bhalla chose to compare Christians to Sikhs, and not to Jains, shows us what result he wanted to arrive at, and nothing more. Since the basic premises on which Bhalla rests his case are flawed, the talking points he derives from them – like the number of conversions per year and the cost per conversion – also fall apart. Tony Joseph concludes that it is difficult to escape the conclusion that Bhalla has tortured his data to make it say what he wants to hear.

Bhalla does not keep silent on Tony Joseph's response. He once again retorts through another article in *The Indian Express* on 5 September 2015 to prove his point. Christian population had declined 0.29 per cent between 1971 and 1991. What were the factors for the population to remain constant from 1991 and 2011? All indicators such as per capita income, education of women and fertility rates suggest that the growth rate should have declined. There could be other reasons he holds such as decreasing death rate among Christians and large presence of foreign Christians at first and denies them as causes later and attributes the entire growth to conversions (*The Indian Express* 2015).

Analysis

The Hindutva groups argue that having failed to exterminate the Hindu nation militarily, Muslims now seek to do so by procreating at a faster rate. The propaganda is that Muslims eschew family planning, practice polygamy, discourage women from gaining a secular education and encourage customs such as purdah, leaving their women illiterate and traditional. On the other hand, the Hindutva group claims that the Christians are equally responsible for the decline of Hindu population due to religious conversions. The Hindus, therefore, must oppose family planning and either impose monogamy on the Muslims or amend the present Hindu code to enable the Hindus to follow polygamy. To counteract the Christians, there should be an anti-conversion law and *Ghar Wapsi* programmes. It is important and essential for India to remain a Hindu nation. But the communalists have not been able to define what constitutes a Hindu nation. To say that India is a Hindu state may not be right. The mass of people that are called Hindus do not belong to a community of fellowship with numerous castes and subcastes. In fact, as far as religion is considered, the Hindutvavadis have made use of it for politics of power and not to empower marginalized communities within the Hindu fold. Not many Hindus of subaltern classes would say that they are a part of a religion that unites them into a community. Communities in Hinduism are unfortunately made up of castes and subcastes, each one of those antagonistic to the other. One, therefore, wonders the expression 'Hindu growth rate'. One also is made to wonder why the SCs/STs are included in the calculation for population growth in the Hindu category. The census pegs the population of SCs at 16.6 per cent and STs at 8.6 per cent, together forming a quarter of the total population. In the period 2001–2011, the SCs have grown by 20.8 per cent and STs by 23.7 per cent. The data show the total population has witnessed a decadal increase of 17.7 per cent to touch 1.21 billion. This does not seem to worry the Hindutvavadis. Why? Though not treated as a part of the community in social living, the group is able to provide cheap and free labour to caste masters.

Similarly the Muslims and Christians, though both form a community, are not homogenous groups and are not uniform communities. There are communities within the larger community. Within the Muslim fold there are various subcommunities and the percentage of population growth varies among them depending on their economic status. So also with the Christian communities. There is no single homogonous Christian community in India. There are affluent Christians and impoverished Christian communities. There are Christians in Goa, Kerala and Mumbai and there are Christians in Orissa and Chhattisgarh. They are all different. Besides, there are different groups among them affiliated to different kinds of churches. To dub them as a uniform group and heap stereotypes on them is pure politics and un-academic. The growth rate among both the Christian and Muslim communities may have lot to do with their education and social status than religion. Conversions in India have been minimal. There have been perhaps more conversions to Islam, Buddhism and Sikhism than Christianity. Not that one has to be defensive about conversions. The Indian Constitution offers to ever citizen freedom of faith and expression. However, the way the Sangh Parivar makes use of the issue of conversions against Christians sounds irrational. The demographers have also noted that India's Muslim population is unlikely to rise beyond 14 per cent. Hindu radicals still may say that the minorities are going to take over the country. The Muslims' population growth rate in spite of its decline has become just another issue to be manipulated in the radicals' attempt to 'saffronize' India and marginalize the country's minorities. When one closely views the religious figures the country has remained largely immune to the advance of Christianity or Islam. Hinduism has maintained a dominant presence across the country with the exception of Northeast. But the communal rhetoric has been used to serve partisan interests.

Religious Census and Injustice

The country has adopted a constitution based on the principles of secularism and democracy. The Government of India after independence in 1951 had decided not to record any person's caste or race except to the extent necessary for providing information relating to certain disadvantaged groups referred to in the constitution such as the SCs and the STs. Religious census had become important since the constitution has mentioned that no person professing a religion other than Hinduism, Sikhism and Buddhism shall be deemed a member of SC. It was imperative therefore on the part of the census to ask a question on religion in order to determine the SC status of a person. On the other hand, this action was tragic. By excluding those who embrace the two minority religions from the purview of reservation, the Constitution continues to deny SCs their legitimate rights as

SCs. Why should religion, a personal choice an individual makes, deny them their right to their identity as dalits? The Constitution, objectively speaking, has denied justice to SC individuals on conversion to two religions, though their situation may not have changed. Independent India thus has very narrow concept of social justice based on caste within the frame of Hinduism. This decision to exclude dalits on conversion to Islam or Christianity is no doubt communal. Census operations by not publishing the socio-economic data on religion and publishing the demographic data on the other hand has helped in perpetuating demographic communalism. Through census India is projected as a country of six major religious groups, namely, Hindus, Muslims, Christians, Sikhs, Jains and Buddhists concealing the fact that diversity of faiths and practices exist within each of the religious groups of India. Therefore, the process of homogenization of religious communities and religious consolidation continues subtly in independent India which is an attack on India's pluralism.

Do We Need Religious Census?

Given the way the data on religion are misused should the state announce the religious data at all? As a secular state, religion belongs to the personal space and not the public realm. Why should religion become an issue in a secular state? If the data were meant to empower communities or allocation of resources to communities, one could say it was a tolerable exercise. However, one is unsure why the religious demography has become so important other than for purposes of communalism? Besides, the census data on religion gives a misleading picture of the religiosity in the country. This is because of the flawed nature of the census question on religion. There is no one Hinduism in the country. Why dub people of all castes and communities under one nomenclature? Hinduism in the country is plural and cannot be reduced into a single religion. Of course, the caste and religious elites do have a problems when subaltern and discriminated groups make demand for their legitimate right over economic and political resources. Those memories of the demand of the backward classes in accordance with the Mandal Commission in 1990 for 27 per cent reservation had caused fiery protests, rallies, demonstrations and traffic snarls. Students were out on the roads and there were self-immolations. Indra Sawhney, a representative of the elite class, had even filed a PIL in the Supreme Court against the government to put to rest the issue of reservation by seeking a definition of backward classes and whether more than 50 per cent of the seats could be reserved. The recommendation was to offer 27 per cent reservation to 54 per cent, and more of the OBCs and the leaders of the Hindu faith who bracket all Hindus in one category were unwilling to share the country's resources with their Hindu brothers and sisters. The manner in which SCs/STs are treated even to this day as impure and ostracized from social life and economic participation makes one wonder how they can be bracketed into 'Hindu' religion. Reducing different communities into one nomenclature of Hindus, Christians or Muslims gives the impression that these are homogenous communities. Surely they are not. Even some of those who belong to a religion do so because their family brought them up in that faith, not because they still believe in it or actively practice it. Even those who believe in religion consider it personal. The data on religious belief in the census should therefore be viewed as indicative of culture rather than of religion. The data also says nothing about the actual religious practice, involvement, belief or belonging of the population. Religious data therefore create more problems than solve issues. Most countries of the world do not categorize people into religion. The purpose of the census should be to ensure that each community or region get the right number of representatives in government. The data could help the state with the equitable distribution of public funds. In broad terms, the census is meant to help the state to see how country is changing and how the state should respond to those changes every ten years. The information of the census is to help policy makers design new legislations and policies. It is unfortunately used by vested interest groups to further their designs. There needs to be a law to protect census data so that it is not misused.

Conclusion

Among the multiple identities of citizens, religion is something that belongs to the personal space of individuals in most developed countries. It is because the state has given prominence to it that religious identities have been communalized in India. For some people, religious affiliation is purely nominal or used as an identifier to distinguish themselves from members of other religious groups. The issue becomes more complex when we look at caste and its association with religion. For most people in the country, religion is not as important as caste since the religious practices are tied up with caste practices in the family, community or cultural heritage. Most religious practices are caste practices and belief, practice, formal membership, informal affiliation, ritual initiation, doctrinal knowledge, moral sense, core values, or one group is regarded by others becomes important. It is also possible to have religion as an important aspect of personal identity without participating actively, being a formal member of a faith community, or even agreeing with basic tenets of the relevant faith. While religious identities may remain important, in a country like India to dub various castes and communities under Hindu religion may pose a problem. While politically religious categorization has helped some political parties to consolidate vote banks, the category of Hinduism to all other than followers of minority religions may wipe out small traditions, diverse forms of religious expressions of people and communities. What may be worth examining is whether religious identities should be given the importance that they are given at present and should they be homogenized in the way it is done. A secular state while respecting diversity may have to allow the practice of religion to the private space of citizens.

References

http://indianexpress.com/article/opinion/columns/census-christians-conversions

http://indianexpress.com/article/opinion/columns/bend-it-like-bhalla/#sthash.Udoh7ds4.dpuf

Ramavarman, T. 2013. 'Hindu Families Should Have at Least Three Kids: RSS', *The Times of India*, Sunday, October 27.

The Indian Express, 5 September 2015.

Wriggins, W. Howard and James F. Guyot. 1973. 'Demographic Change and Politics: An Introduction', in W. Howard Wriggins and James F. Guyot (eds.), *Population, Politics, and the Future of Southern Asia*, New York: Columbia University Press, p. 6.

7 Muslim Demography and Democracy

J.S. Bandukwala

The process of partition of India began 50 years earlier around 1900. The census figures of 1891 and 1911 may be the spark that split the country. In democracy, power is related to the population numbers that support you. The early census ignited the fears of Hindu and Muslim leaders. In the United Provinces, Muslim zamindars realized that a Muslim population of barely 14 per cent implied that sooner or later power would flow away from them. These zamindars were the children of Mughal aristocracy and had seen the downfall of the Mughals after 1857. They realized the importance of having a separate Muslim homeland. That required dividing the country or its provinces on the basis of religion. The idea of separation germinated at this stage and was to prove disastrous in 1947.

The same thing happened on the other side. Pandit Madan Mohan Malaviya saw a slight relative fall in Hindu population between 1891 and 1911. It may have been the result of middle class/middle caste migration from India, to East Africa and South East Asia, caused by famine conditions here.

The fear of a Muslim majority, led to the rise of the Hindu Mahasabha, and later the RSS. Oddly even today, after the details of the 2011 census, there are experts who predict that the Muslim population will exceed the Hindu population after 450 years. They go into details of Muslim men having four wives, and twenty-five children. When political heavyweights, such as the late Bal Keshav Thackeray would utter these words, people would believe it, and the poison of hate spreads. Yet studies show that polygamy rate is highest among Buddhists and tribals, then come Jains, then caste Hindus, and lower down is Muslims.

This is understandable as poverty is more widespread among Muslims, and which woman would marry a man who cannot support his earlier wives and children. More relevant at present is the fall in fertility due to the economic well-being of a family. As Muslim poverty levels are high, fertility is high. But as their socio-economic levels rise, fertility will go down. It is absurd to make a 450-year projection based on fertility rates today. It only generates fear and panic among the majority community and leads to hatred for the minority. That is why we must view with concern the meeting of RSS leaders at Raipur, in the thick of the Bihar elections in October 2015, to discuss the slight fall in Hindu percentage over the decade by 0.77 per cent, with a rise of 0.70 per cent among Muslims. One can always speculate whether this Muslim population fears are genuine, or just a pretext to win a crucial election.

The success of secularism in India is vital to the very survival of India as a political unit. That requires an acceptance of pluralism by the general public as well as by the political class. Sadly our people hardly know each other. Most Hindus are unaware that Islam came to India about 629 AD, during the life of the Prophet Muhammad. This was due to trading links between Arabia and the Indian West Coast. Islam had a deep impact on Hinduism. The reverse was also true. Islamic egalitarian spirit loosened the rigidity of caste, and led to the Bhakti movement. This produced some of the greatest Indians of the Middle Ages, such as Kabir, Guru Nanak and Akbar. It led to a cultural and spiritual flowering, unprecedented in our history.

Islam too was substantially effected by Hinduism. Muslim converts did not abandon their caste identities and even prejudices on accepting Islam. This is best illustrated by Ashraf Ali Thanvi, a leading ulema and scholar of the nineteenth century, who classified Muslims into three categories: Ashraf (meaning noble), Ajlaf (meaning contemptible) and Arzal (meaning ignoble) for dalit and poor Muslims.

Note that equality is a cornerstone of Islam, and such categorization was itself a violation of Islam. No wonder most lower caste and dalit conversions occurred under the spiritual influence of Sufi saints, such as Khwaja Moinuddin Chisti, who preached that all are creations of the One God. But the caste rigidity within converted upper caste Muslims alienated the dalits and lower castes. The process of conversion stopped. This explains why India was the only country, in the vast region from Morocco to Indonesia, that did not have a majority Muslim population.

The future of India is tied to our capacity to rise above our religious and caste differences. Can we treat all Indians as our brothers and sisters? Can we inculcate a scientific and rational thinking among our 1.3 billion people? Should the government be concerned about what Indians eat or dress or read? Or to put it more bluntly is the life of one Indian worth much less than the life of a cow? This is the land of Gandhi, Nanak and Kabir. This country will survive because of the blessings of these great souls.

8 Demographic Profile of Parsi Population in India

Some Concerns

U.V. Somayajulu

Zoroastrianism is one of world's oldest monotheistic religions. They worship in fire temples and believe fire represents God's light or wisdom. The Zoroastrians believe that there is one God called Ahura Mazda (Wise Lord). This was founded by Zoroaster, also known as Zarathustra, in Persia about 3,500 years ago. It was once one of world's most powerful religions, it is now one of the smallest. Zoroastrians are roughly split into two groups, Iranians and Parsis. Parsi means Persian.

Sometime after the beginning of eighth century, a group of Zoroastrians fled Iran and arrived on India's west coast and settled in Gujarat. In the seventeenth century, migrated to Mumbai, where they built their fire temples. Most of India's Parsis live in Mumbai, where statues and buildings pay homage to glorious past when Parsis were a dominant force as traders and shipbuilders, administrators and wealthy philanthropists. Zoroastrians are roughly split into two groups, Iranians and Parsis.

An attempt is made in this chapter to understand the demographic profile of Parsi population in India in terms of population growth, marriages, fertility, migration and so on. The chapter is based on the secondary data and publications of Indian census and other sources including the research work done by demographers/scholars.

Parsi Community

Parsis of India are unique community, but their numbers are declining fast. Many famous persons such as Tata and Godrej, distinguished lawyers and politicians belong to this community. Tata, group's unique character, was shaped by passions of its founder Jamsetji Tata and his successors. Jamsetji was born in 1839 into a Parsi family, with his forefathers being Zoroastrian priests.

The Parsis first arrived escaping persecution in Iran, as refugees from Pars (Persia), by boat to Sanjan, a small town in Gujarat in the eighth century (936 CE).

'At that point of time, our fore fathers didn't have any navigation systems. The sea winds brought us to these shores because God thought that if our community were to survive, Gujarat in India was the place where we could flourish', says the patriarch of the last surviving family troupe of Parsi theatre performers in Gujarati.

Before refugees could make Gujarat their home, Jaditya Rana, local monarch, questioned the head priest on how they planned to reside in an already over populated place.

Nairyosang Dhawal, leader of the refugees, called for a bowl of milk and a spoonful of sugar, carefully blended sugar into milk, without spilling a drop and added that Parsis will blend with local population like sugar in milk and sweeten the society. Pleased with answer, Rana promised them a home. They adopted Gujarati as their mother tongue and their women began to dress in saris.

Once they found their feet, industrious and business-minded Parsis flourished in Gujarat and inhabited towns and villages of Gujarat making their living as farmers, weavers, carpenters and bakers.

Parsi Population Trends

The exact number of Parsis living across the world is not known but one estimate as on 2004 gives a range of

124,000–190,000,with about half of them living in India. One estimate puts the Parsi population around the globe as 110,000. In 2006, *New York Times* reported that there were less than 190,000 Zoroastrians worldwide. Another estimate puts the Parsi population in the world to be 138,000. Thus, there is no clarity with regard to the estimated Parsi population across the globe.

Table 8.1 gives the Parsi population in different countries.

Table 8.1 *Parsi Population by Country*

Country	*Time*	*Estimate*
Iran		15,000–24,000
United Kingdom	2004	5,000
Australia and New Zealand	2004	3,000
North America	2004	15,500
Pakistan	2010	1,766
India	2001	69,601
Elsewhere	2010	2,500
Total		112,367–121,367

Parsi Population in India

The estimate for India was 60,000 Parsis, half the number in 1940s. In a population of 1.2 billion in India, there are about 69,000 Parsis. The 2001 census recorded a 21 per cent decadal growth of the country's population, but the number of Parsis declined in each decade since 1941. 2001 Census recorded 21 per cent decadal growth of country's population, while number of Parsis declined by about 12 per cent each decade since 1941.

Table 8.2 *Parsi Population in India 1881–2001*

Census Year	*No of Parsis*	*Decennial Change (%)*
1881	85,078	
1891	89,490	+5.19
1901	93,617	+4.61
1911	99,412	+6.19

Cont'd...

...Cont'd

1921	101,075	+1.67
1931	108,988	+7.83
1941	114,890	+5.42
1951*	111,791	-0.27
1961	100,772	-10.93
1971	91,266	-10.42
1981	71,630	-27.41
1991	76,382	+6.63
2001	69,601	-9.74

*The drop in population reflects the loss of 5,000 Parsis to Pakistan after the Partition of British India.

Reasons for Decline in Parsi Population

As per the National Commission for Minorities, there are many reasons for steady decline in the population of Parsi community in India (Taraporevala 2000). One-fifth of decrease in Parsi population is attributed to migration (Unisa, Bhagat and Roy 2004). Slower birth rate than death rate accounts for the rest. Childlessness and migration emerge as the major factors followed by low levels of fertility, and changes in marriage patterns including intermarriage, non-marriage and late marriage.

For instance, according to Directory of Surat Parsi Panchayat, city's Parsi population was 3,584 in 2014, against 3,616 in 2004 and 3,696 in 2010.

For every Parsi born, four die and decline in numbers is attributed to late marriage, no marriage, or mixed marriage with non-Parsis. The Parsi community is the more westernized than other societies in India. They delay marriage while they save or wait for property. The Parsi couples began family planning decades ago to ensure that they pay for education of children, considered important for girls as well as boys.

Delayed or No Marriage

Parsi women are high achievers at work and they are reluctant to marry and start family at an early age, and being

single is socially acceptable in the Parsi community. Roy, Unisa and Bhatt (2004) found that in Greater Mumbai where the density of Parsis is highest, about 10 per cent of Parsi females and about 20 per cent of Parsi males did not marry.

In 1881, as per Bombay Parsi Panchayat records, more than half of the marriages in Bombay were before girl was 15 years, while 10 per cent were when girl was above 20 years. In era of child marriages, Parsis were the first in India to abandon this. By 1890, most of the Parsi women in Bombay married between 16 and 20 years, and by 1901, almost half of them married at 20+ years. By 1930, median age of marriage for Parsi women was 24 years. Such jump in marriage age indicated sweeping social change that gave Parsi women greater freedom and access to education and employment.

Non-marriage was not a trend that was confined to urban Bombay as studies conducted in rural Gujarat indicated that 13 per cent to 55 per cent of women in rural Gujarat continued to be never married well into their middle age.

Malini Karkal's (1982) Bombay Parsi Panchayat commissioned study in 1982 indicated that 21 per cent of the Parsi females of 40–49 years were unmarried, while 68 per cent of women of 20–29 years were never married. In 1971, 19 per cent of the general population of Greater Bombay and 6 per cent of the general population in Maharashtra were never married. She warned that proportion of unmarried individuals was increasing among the Parsi community and noted that as per 1971 census, only 0.58 per cent of all the Indian females in the same cohort were unmarried. Unisa, Bhagat and Roy (2004) found that one of five Parsi Indian males, and one of ten females, was unmarried by 50 years of age.

Fertility

Parsi birth rate was below the replacement level by 1961, necessary to sustain community's population. According to Leela Visaria (1972), as per the 1881 census, first comprehensive census Parsi fertility rates were 'moderately high' with 34 per 1,000 population for Parsis in Bombay. This declined to 14 per 1,000 by late 1940s (Chandra Sekar's study, 1948) and continued to decline. By 1960s, the fertility rate reached 12 per 1,000 for Parsis against 38 per 1,000 in case of general population in 1970.

According to Leela Visaria (1974), because of late marriage or non-marriage, births to Parsi women of Greater Bombay in 1961 were only 50 per cent of the number that would have occurred if every woman were married throughout her reproductive period. By 1980–1982, TFR for Parsis was 1.12, about half of replacement level. In 2000, it was 0.9425. Zubin Shroff's (2011) demographic study of Parsis using data from 2001–2006 observed TFR of 0.88.

Demographic Characteristics of Parsis

The sex ratio among Parsis is unusual, as the ratio of males to females was 1,000 males to 1,050 females in 2001 (up from 1,024 in 1991) and this is primarily due to the higher median age of the population (elderly women are more common than elderly men). This was 1,000 males to 933 females in 2001 at the national level.

Parsis have higher literacy rate with 98 per cent literacy rate in 2001, the highest of any Indian community (the national average was 65%). About 96 per cent of the Parsis reside in urban areas (against the national average of 28%).

Age Structure

In 1881, 37 per cent of Parsi population of India was 14 years and below, while 5 per cent was of 60+ years. By 1971, 15 per cent population in Greater Bombay (now home to overwhelming majority of the Parsis) was of 14 years and below, while 60+ years aged was 20 per cent. In 1999, Singh and Gowri found that median age of Parsi population surveyed was 48 years, against 24 years as per 1901 census. According to Unisa et al. (2009), in 2001 one in every eight Parsis was under 15 years, one in four Parsis was 65 years and above. Percentage of 65+ population was higher than that of Japan, Spain and Sweden. United Nations defines a population aged if more than 7 per cent of the population is above 65 years. Proportion of aged Parsis is over *triple* of this.

Projections

Demographic projections indicate that by 2020, the Parsi population would reach 23,000. Then Parsis might be called as a tribe instead of community Unisa et al. (2009) projected that by 2051, only 32,000 Parsis will be in India. Shroff estimated that Parsi population of Mumbai will decline from 46,557 in 2001 to 20,122, while about 70,000 Parsis called Bombay home in 1971.

With current rates of fertility and intermarriage, in 2051 Parsi population in Mumbai will be:

19,136 if no children of any intermarried couple are accepted
20,122 if only children of intermarried women are excluded
20,535 if all children of intermarriages are accepted

Concerns and Initiatives

Of late, concerns are raised over rapidly declining population of Parsi community in India. The anxiety about disappearing population intensified debate about who can be counted as Parsi. More than one-third of Parsis marry non-Parsis. Children of Parsi men will always be Parsi whoever he weds, but if a Parsi woman marries outside the community, her sons and daughters are not deemed Parsis.

Singh and Gowri (1999) asked the Parsis in over 6,000 Mumbai households about causes for their decreasing numbers. About 81 per cent reported intermarriage as the major cause, while 74 per cent mentioned migration outside India. Half of them believed that conversion to other religions was a serious problem.

Intermarriages

Intermarriages within the community have become far more common, says Dinyar Patel (2011). According to an estimate, close to 30 per cent of Parsis in the bigger cities such as Mumbai, Delhi and Pune are marrying outside the community. It doesn't only have to do with educational qualifications or money, it also emerges from a dearth of like-minded people within the community. Today's teenagers are not weighed down by the stigma that was attached to marrying outside the community in the 70s and the 80s.

One woman married a Hindu in 1993, until 2003 nobody stopped her from attending fire temple or Towers of Silence, place Parsis consign their dead, in Valsad, Gujarat, where her parents live. Local Parsi panchayat, an administrative body, has decided that women like her are not welcome at those holy places. Her biggest fear is that she will not be allowed to attend the last rites when her elderly parents die:

> The thought my parents would be no more tomorrow and I would not be allowed to enter is like mentally abusing a woman, the thought is very unpleasant for me. We are three sisters married to non-Parsis. So, none of us would be able to attend if this continues. It is like bullying people. Who gives them the right to do that? This is sex discrimination and women are fighting it in courts for five years.

Jiyo Parsi campaign is considered to have limited impact as couples would qualify for assistance if husband is Parsi.

'Sorry as one might feel at a personal level, they need to recognise that if they have chosen to marry out, they have broken rules of religious customs and practices. There is a price one pays for it', according to Trustee of Bombay Parsi Panchayat, and founder of Zoroastrian Studies, organization dedicated to disseminating information about religion.

According to a Parsi leader:

> If we want to preserve Parsi ethnic identity, marrying out is not the answer. If we turn a blind eye to our kids marrying out, then I do not see Zoroastrianism surviving into next century. These people are breaking down something we preserved for 3,500 years, they are destroying fabric of community existence.

Initiatives

'I want them to survive' says Minister of Minority Affairs, Najma Heptulla. In an effort to change this, the government is spending $1.5 m to encourage them to have more children.

To reverse the decline in Parsi population, community bodies are providing affordable housing, one factor that deters many Parsis from getting married, to aspirational youth. Surat Parsi Panchayat rents out homes to young Parsis who promise to marry other Parsis and start a family, at rock bottom rentals.

'The community takes care of us if we think of larger good. Ever since we enter our teenage, our parents drill it in our heads that we should marry only a good Parsi boy. In many cases, the panchayat plays an active part in the marriage itself' said one Parsi girl.

'Reversing the population decline won't be easy for the community. It will involve a change in social attitudes for sure. Over the past few decades, many Parsis chose to have fewer or no children' says Dinyar Patel, a historian and PhD candidate.

The Mumbai-based organization Zoroastrian Youth for the Next Generation (ZYNG) hosts youth meets where Parsi boys and girls get to know each other. The programmes are designed with the ostensible purpose of breaking the ice between the sexes, so that eventually one of them takes the initiative and they get married. Apart from workshops that focus on the tenets of Zoroastrianism and light-hearted entertainment, they also have cheesy sessions such as *Love, Sex Aur Dhokha*.

Concluding Remarks

Decline in Parsi population is a concern and the government is spending on housing for Parsis. Ageing among the Parsis is another concern besides mental health status and issues. The efforts being made by the government as well as the Parsi community groups and panchayats seem to be inadequate. We need more intensive efforts and initiatives to address the related issues. Also the concerns of the community members, particularly the youth, need attention from the

Parsi Panchayat as well as the government. We also need update data on the Parsi population and its profile. For instance, census 2011 data on the Parsi population is still awaited. We also need data on out migration of Parsis from India. The situation could be similar in case of other religious groups with smaller size and needs to be studied.

References

Karkal, Malini. 1982. *Survey of Parsi Population of Greater Bombay*, Mumbai: Report of International Institute of Population Studies.

Patel, Dinyar. 2011. 'Understanding Parsi Population Decline in India: A Historical Perspective', *Jawaharlal Nehru Centre*, Mumbai, 7 May.

Roy, T.K., Unisa, S. and Bhat, M. 2004. *Growth of the Parsi Population in India*, Mumbai: National Commission for Minorities.

Sekar, C. Chandra. 1948. 'Some Aspects of Parsi Demography', *Human Biology*, Vol. 20, May.

Shroff, Zubin and Marcia C. Castro. 2011. The potential impact of intermarriage on the population decline of the Parsis of Mumbai, India, in *Demographic Research*, Vol. 25, Article 17, pp. 545–564.

Singh, D.P. and V.G. Gowri. 2000. *Parsis of Mumbai: A Socio-Demographic Profile*, Mumbai: Report of Tata Institute of Social Sciences.

Taraporevala, S. 2000. *Zoroastrians of India. Parsis: A Photographic Journey*, Bombay: Good Books.

Unisa, Sayeed, R.B. Bhagat and T.K. Roy. 2004. 'Demographic Predicament of Parsis in India', Paper Presented at XXVI International Population Conference, Marrakech, 27 September–2 October.

Visaria, Leela. 1972. *Religious and Regional Differences in Mortality and Fertility in the Indian Subcontinent*, PhD Dissertation submitted to Princeton University.

Visaria, Leela. 1974. 'Demographic Transition among Parsis: 1881–1971' (Three parts), *Economic and Political Weekly*, Vol. 10, 12 October, 19 October, 26 October.

9 Kandhamal Riot

Role of Demographic Composition, Manipulation of Identity and Communal Polarization

Himanshu Sekhar Mishra

With the murder of Sri Lakshmananda Saraswati – one of the leaders of Vishwa Hindu Parishad on 23 August 2008, Kandhamal riot began. While Maoist insurgents were blamed by the police, on the other hand, some Hindu organizations suspected a secret agreement between Christian missionaries and the Pana (dalit) caste. This gave rise to a riot between the indigenous Kandha tribe (largely Hindu) and the Christian minority amongst the Pana caste. Justice S.C. Mohapatra said in his interim report on the violence in Kandhamal that 'The violence in Kandhamal was the result of concentrated discontentment prevailing among the people since long. They relate to conversion, re-conversion; land-grabbing and non-maintenance of land records; and fake certificate issues' ('Kandhamal Lies Nailed' 2009). However, this chapter without denying Mohapatra's committee report on Kandhamal riot reports that the main reason of riot was manipulation of demography and religious identity of local communities by the extreme forces.

Demographic Composition of Kandhamal

Kandhamal District is one of the backward districts of Orissa whose headquarter is at Phulbani. This district is bounded by Boudh district in the north, Rayagada district in the south, Ganjam district and Nayagarh district in the east and Kalahandi district in the west. Kandhamal is one of the newly created districts carved out of the old Phulbani district. It was formed on 1 January 1994. The name of the district 'Kandhamal' is derived from the name of its majority inhabitants 'Kandhas'. However, besides them, there are different STs and SCs divided across different religions and non-religion/animism. This chapter deals with the demographic composition of major communities (related to riot) in Kandhamal and with interaction and interrelation between these communities with one another.

Kandhas

Kandhas constitute 93.33 per cent of the total tribal population (51.96% of total population) of Kandhamal district. The name which they use themselves is 'Ku' and their language should accordingly be dominated as 'Kui'. With the march of time, these tribes have accepted the name 'Kond', 'Khond', 'Kondh' and 'Kandha' as conferred upon them by non-tribals. Historically, after the fall of Harappan culture, the ancestors of Kandhas with other inhabitants marched towards Gangetic valley and started their settlement at the feet of Himalayas. Then due to some unknown reasons, they left the foot of the Himalayas in two groups. One group marched towards the east and other group to the south and settled in the soil of Odisha through Vindhya Mountains. In this connection, there is a folk song of Titlagarh region which says that the ancestors of Kandhas were settled at the Himalayas and then at Vindhya Hill ranges '*Himalaya ra andh, binja giri ra Kandha, Athe jelen Kandhen, Basalya kalasur mandh*' (Ratha 2010: 7). It is believed that the Kandhas migrated from Madhya Pradesh and entered into the district of Kalahandi and divided into two divisions. The branch which took south-east direction might have proceeded to Belghar region, the south-west of Kandhamal district (Ratha 1993). The Kandhas for the first time settled in Sapangada of Tumudibandha block. Thereafter, they established their settlement at Adanga Pata and Sujunga Pata. The ensuing Kandha legend tells that prior to the settlement in this district, it was occupied by the Kurumas who were a peace-loving community. They were domiciled in Paberi, Ghodapathar, Linepada, Purangada, Kainjhar of Khajuripada, Chakapad and Tikabali blocks. After a skirmish with Kandhas, the Kurumas were forced out from this land and subsequently they migrated to the neighbouring districts Ganjam and Daspalla of present Nayagarh district. Thereafter, Kandhamal became the strong hold of the Kandhas.

The ethnic composition of Kandha is so diversified in terms of rites, social customs, economy and even language (Schulze 1911; Winfield 1929) that any single name to encompass this complexity would be seen inappropriate (Pathy 1995). Ethnographers of Kandha community have divided them into several categories such as Kutia, Dongria and Desia. These categories are overlapping and heterogeneous in nature. Some of the categories such as Desia Kandha are further subdivided into Raj Kandha with landed property, Dal Kandha as Hinduized Kandha and Pakhia Kandha who eat buffalo flesh and grow turmeric (Pathy 1995; Russell and Hiralal 1916).

Kandhas in real sense do not belong to any mainstream religious community since they practise 'animism':

> Nature (Prakriti) is their religion. They believe the divine does not reside in the temple, mosque, church or any other houses of worship, built by man. They believe that whenever, they want to meet him, he will appear before them. They are taught that the divine can be summoned and he never betrays his devotees. And the devotee does not have to go to special prayer hall or structure to meet him. (K.B. 2008: 21)

Pana in Kandhamal

From among SC population (16.89% of total population), Pana constitutes largest non-tribal community whose percentage is 77.92. B.B. Mohanty in order to trace out origin and history of Pana quoted the opinions of Russell and Hiralal that the word Pana is derived from the term 'Panka', a Dravidian caste of weaver and labourers (Senapati and Kunar 1980). The Pana migrated to Kandhamal from the nearby 'Ghumusar area as the king there punished them because of their criminal activities' (Mohanty, N.R. 2008; and also Lenin Kumar 2008: 63). Pana had been living with Kandha more than 200 years in jungle (Pathy 1995). They had been tied with Kandha in terms of language, social practice, festivals and other rituals. The Pana women have tattoo like Kandha women over their body. Panas have been observing some rites and customs of Kandhas in occasion of birth, death and marriage. They also participate in the worshipping of Dharani Penu. Some Kandhas have also learnt Oriya from Panas. They have started using colourful napkins by learning from Panas. These are many examples where one can find that there have been two-way cultural interactions between Kandhas and Panas.

Hindus in Kandhamal

Hindus as immigrants have been staying in Kandhamal for 350 years. They constitute 81.42 per cent of total population. 350 Years ago, some of the kings from the plains managed to send some of their subjects to curb the resistance struggle of the Kandha and protect their own frontiers from Kandha raids and guerrilla warfare. These immigrants established a few fortified and separate settlements in the hills (Pathy 1976, 1995) and gradually expand their domination beyond the Hindu settlements. In the twentieth century, the feelings of nationalism became dominant in the subcontinental area. The realm of Kandhas fell in the region of Orissa/Kalinga, and Oriya nationalism (mostly Hindu nationalism) took over their identities. But, this was not necessarily a negative relationship. In fact, people living in the plains of Kalinga, since ancient times, had forged a syncretic culture with those living in the dense forest of the regions (K.B. 2008: 21).

In the postcolonial period, many people migrated from coastal Odisha to Kandhamal as this region is full of resources and opportunities. Similarly, some people migrated from Bihar to Kandhamal. The higher caste communities of Kandhamal comprised Odias and non-Odias. These higher caste people in Kandhamal are Brahmins, Karan, Khandayat, Teli, Paika, Gauda and Bania. These people as a whole are known as 'Odia' by the original inhabitants of Kandhamal. Most of the land approximately 32 per cent is occupied by them. While Odia migrants have dominated over the land, administration, education, health and politics, non-Odia migrants have total control over business, land and politics. Both these migrants live in the mainstream urban or semi-urban area. They consider themselves modern, civilized and affluent.

Christianity in Kandhamal

From among many denominations of Indian Christianity in Odisha, three denominations, that is, Catholic, Protestant and Pentecostal churches are very active. Initially, they all were in costal Orissa. When philanthropic activities of missionaries were not able to influence much people in coastal Orissa during their early days of presence in Orissa, Christianity shifted their strategy to the hilly tracts of Orissa. Administrator J. Campbell was very keen to welcome them into Kandhamal (Pathy 1995: 227). However, overall they constitute 18.2 per cent of total population of Kandhamal. In Kandhamal, there has been a rivalry between Catholic and Protestant denominations. Catholic Christianity believes that the priest (Father) is the mediator between God and human beings. They run big churches on the principles of chain of command. Conversely, Protestants believe in the trinity of god. They never believe in conversion based on proselytization. They believe that people should follow Christianity through inner realization. While among Panas, there are more converts to Catholicism; Kandhas tend to convert to Protestantism.

Interaction and Relation between Communities

As it is mentioned earlier, Kandhas are major and original inhabitants of Kandhamal and later on Odias (Hindus), Panas, Christians/missionaries and Hindutva forces came there later. As a result, Kandhas interacted with Panas, Hindus and Christians and they all interacted with one another. Manipulation begins when interaction starts.

Kandhas and Hindus Relationship and Hinduization Process

One can say that, there was a silent Hinduization process in Kandhamal since no one was systematically and intentionally proselytizing people. Many areas of Kandha life such as material, religious, economic, social and linguistic aspects have been affected by the Hindu culture since their contact dates back to hundreds of years. During the Bhanja dynasty, Hindus had considerable influence on Kondhs because of their close and intimate interaction with them. Many customs, habits and practice of caste Hindus were observed by Kondhs and in course of time, they made those into their part of culture (Behera 1996: 58). In this period, moneylenders (mostly Hindus) and Kandhas were visiting to one another's houses. The caste Hindus also established kinship with Kandhas and they addressed each other as 'mita' (ritual friend). Kandha people also got an opportunity to explore Hindu practices from them. Gradually, Kandhas depended more on other caste communities in Kandhamal for day-to-day activities of agricultural operation. For this purpose, a type of 'jajmani relationship' was established with different caste groups of the locality (ibid.: 138). Here jajmani relationship refers to inter-cast service relationship. The Kandha have to depend on *lohar* (blacksmith) for repairing and sharpening their iron implements and on *kumbhar* (potter) for getting earthen pots.

However, the process of systematic Hinduization in Kandhamal was first started by colonial bureaucracy, headed by Hindu higher castes. British administration appointed Hindu higher caste people in different regions.

Consequently, the higher caste started to dominate not only in the administrative spheres of Kandha life but also in its social and cultural life. Hinduization began with drives to build Hindu temples in parts of western Orissa.

Here one can specifically refer to the temple building project of the Tahasildar Dinabandhu Patnaik. The scheme involved building Siva Mandir (Siva temple) in 1855 at Bisipara. This was Patnaik's head quarter. In fact, this was not built only by the people of Bisipara, but by the people of Kandhamal region, through beti (unpaid labour) (Pati 2001).

With the emergence of Swami Laxmanananda Saraswati in Kandhamal, Hinduization process got geared up which was involved with many forms of manipulations.

Changing Trend in Kandhas – Panas Relationship

When Pana came to Kandhamal, Kandha welcomed them and gave them shelter in their village and they in turn acted as mediator between Kandhas and Oriyas and worked as weavers and petty traders (Pathy 1976, 1995; Thiady 1965). Along with it, they were performing two functions: first, they were working as serfs to Kandhas. So 'Kandha raja, Pana praja' was the popular catch phrase of the time and it has been prevailing till today (Lingaraja 2008; Mohanty 2008; second, they were working as the *Meriah* provider to Kandhas for which they were given land as reward for their service to Kandhas (Mohapatra and Bhattacharya 1996). *Meriah* practice, to Kandhas, is a tradition where they killed a child for their betterment. The Kandha never used anybody of their own community as a *Meriah*. So, Panas acted as brokers who were supplying *Meriah* child to the tribal community. However, Panas failed to supply *Meriah* child, they even sacrificed their children for the *Meriah* practice to appease mother goddess (Mohanty, S.C., 2008).

F.G. Bailey has noted the following about the relations between Kandhas (whom he refers to as Kond) and Panas (whom he refers to as PAN):

> The correct traditional behaviour between a Kond and a PAN symbolizes their relative political and economic status. The PAN takes cooked food and water from a Kond: but a Kond cannot take these things from a PAN without being polluted. A PAN may not enter a Kond house, because his presence would pollute it and render necessary a ritual cleansing. Equally a Kond will not go into a PAN house, though in this case it is not the house which is polluted but the intruder. Touch defiles. The Kond addresses a PAN as 'son' or 'child' while the latter must reciprocate with 'father'. A PAN squats to converse with a Kond, if the latter is standing: or the Kond sits on a verandah, while the PAN must squat in the street. The PANS live in their own ghettoes. Their houses are smaller and meaner than most of the houses of the clean castes, and in the old street which adjoins Baderi hamlet the houses are crammed close together. The PANS may not use the village wells or bathing place, because they would bring pollution. Every aspect of their lives reveals the PANS in a position of ritual and social inferiority. (1960: 134)

However, this social order between Kandhas and Panas was transformed by the activities of British administration/Christian missionary and Hindutva group which will be dealt later. Presently, the bone of contention between the two communities was the sphere of local power and question of status in the village hierarchy. Pana did not see their future in the old Kandha-dominated social hierarchy (Mohapatra and Bhattacharya 1996). They perceived that their future was outside this order and in the larger area of politics and society. Since 1950s, dalit assertion and identity has obtained centre stage in the Phulbani politics. The year 1994 was a turning point in the Kandhamal political history. Kandhamal Vikas Parishad (KVP) took birth in the middle of 1994. It articulated the problems of the Kandha tribals. It won 1995 assembly election in Phulbani while defeating Janata Dal, backed by Pana candidate, which accentuated the process of tribal reassertion and political mobilization. The infighting within the Janata Dal leaders was the result of 1994 Pana–Kandha violence. Kamalakanta Pandey, a Brahmin, of Janata Dal had a bitter relationship with

Padmanabha Behera (a dalit Pana Janata Dal leader), and this was a factor responsible for violence. He propagated hatred against Pana community, stimulated Kandha–Pana friction and took the leadership of 1994 Pana–Kandha violence (Roul 2014).

Discrimination at political level has provided an impetus to the conflict. The Representation of the People Act sanctioned two assembly constituencies, one for tribals and one for dalits in Kandhamal. The dalit MLA has been obtaining ministership in every state cabinet, regardless of who is in the power: Congress, Janata Dal or BJD (Lingaraja 2008).

In 1981, the state government forwarded a recommendation to central government, seeking tribal status to Kui-speaking Pana Christians (Lingaraja 2008: 36). In 1991, Pana Christian elite leaders formed Phulbani Kui Jana Kalyana Sangha (PKJS) at Bhubaneswar, whose office bearers were all Panas (Lingaraja 2008: 36). The PKJS started vigorous campaign for providing ST status to Kui-speaking Pana Christians at different levels. They claimed that their language is Kui. They said that they too dwelt in the forests until the government notified them as SCs in 1956. Further, they asserted 'we have the same festivals, the same marriage and death rituals. We have the same mother tongue, i.e. Kui, so why should we not be considered as tribals' (*Times of India*, Delhi Edition, October 12, 2008: 12).

The Land Transfer Act of 1971 categorically states that Panas are recognized as hill tribes. Even in 1936, the union government had said that though Panas throughout Odisha be classified as SCs, those in Kandhamal should be exempted from this and be considered as tribals. The people's mobilization by PKJS generated cultural backing to obtain the ST status. On the other hand, the Kandha community got angry over this development. The Kandha leaders of Phulbani Kui Samanya Samiti (PKSS), a tribal forum, decided to counter PKJS in an aggressive manner. They saw it as a forum of Panas to encroach on their language in order to claim ST status. Mainly, three fears gripped the Kandha mind: fear of losing linguistic identity, fear of assimilation on linguistic line and fear of marginalization with regard to resources. Consequently, tribals took to violence several times to disassociate Panas from their claim (Roul 2014).

With the demand of ST status by Pana Christians on the claim of having same culture as Kandha especially in language, Kandhas started a direct conflict with Panas who, they believed, had fraudulently sought to become competitors in their legitimate entitlement. The Kandhas were afraid that their current access to opportunities would be substantially curtailed if the Panas, with their better education and exposure, were made to compete with them. The Kandhas were determined not to allow this under any circumstances (Mohanty, N.R., 2008).

Gender too was a major issue of contention between Kandha and Pana conflict. Rape and molestation are two serious crimes that emerged in the mid-1990s in Kandhamal. During the year 1990–1995, 70 rapes had taken place and most of the victims were Kandhas and Panas. The number of rape victims among Kandha women was higher than of Pana women. In case of rape, the offenders were contractors, police personnel, government officials and forest officials. Sometimes, they paid huge money to Pana boys to kidnap the Kandha girls. It is also witnessed that they showed the false dream of marriage to Kandha girls and raped repeatedly. When the tension prevailed in the tribal community, these officials started blaming the Pana community for rape and they proved themselves innocent (Roul 2014). Kandha women were also raped by Pana people. The Pana youth was more likely to molest a Kandha girl than vice versa. This was a very important aspect of Kandha–Pana conflict in Kandhamal.

Kandhas Relation with Christian Missionaries

The main motive of Christian missionaries in Kandhamal was conversion. They first studied the rites and rituals of Kandhas and found that without offering them education, Christianity cannot reach them. Through social reforms, the missionaries first started to eliminate the practice of *Meriah* killing in Kandhamal with the help of British administration which was stiffly opposed by Kandha community. Along with it, missionaries also tried to abolish child marriage, polygamous marriage, joint family, dormitory life, tattoo mark over the face of girls and women, bride price, tribal traditional dress and ornaments and other traditional tribal practices. When British administrators such as John Campbell and S.C. Macpherson banned *Meriah* practice and raided many Kandha houses (Pathy 1995, Padel 1995) and rescued the *Meriah* children, it led to a fierce fight between British administration and Kandhas for a prolonged period of 20 years from 1835 to 1855. The Kandha also led a powerful movement against British policy, for example, 'In 1865, the Kutia Kandha revolted against police excesses and forced unpaid labour for construction of roads during agricultural seasons' (Pathy 1995: 226). With the prohibition of *Meriah* practice by British government and dissatisfaction of Kandhas and their subsequent boycotting British administration. Missionaries too got frustrated and started their ways of manipulation, which will be dealt later.

Panas and Christianity

Interaction of Panas with Christianity and British administration made a shift in Kandha and Pana relationship. Earlier, British administration employed Panas to clear forests and roads, construct buildings and railway works and work in paper industries, and paid them higher wages, and on the other hand, introduced new land relations that deprived the Kandhas of their traditional rights over the forest land. It was the policy of divide and rule of Britishers which pushed Panas to embrace Christianity and Kandhas partly due to their commitment to their own culture, that the Kandhas have a history of vociferous resistance to religious conversion by missionaries. Consequently, Kandhas started hating Panas who were closer to Christianity and blamed them as traitors to their old religion and society. After the Panas conversion to Christianity and their interaction with the market economy during, in post-independence period, they got government jobs and become moneylenders (Mohapatra and Bhattacharya 1996). A few Panas took advantage of moneylending and got the Kandha lands mortgaged and thus Kandhas lost their land to Panas. Some Pana petty-bourgeoisie started to cheat Kandhas in several ways. Some notorious Panas started to steal goats, hens and cows of Kandhas. These kinds of incidents also annoyed Kandhas (Kumar 2008).

The Khond purchased the *Meriah* victims. Unless brought with a price, they were not deemed acceptable to the Goddess earth (Taru Penu). Victims from their own tribe were not procurable. The agents, mainly Panas ... sometimes purchased but more frequently kidnapped the children (from outside) whom they sold to Khonds. They occasionally (even) sold their (Khonds) own offspring without any hesitation (Swaro 1990).

The Kandhas felt that the Panas who were their dependents at one time were land owners, and thus for the Kandhas, the Panas became exploiters and land snatchers (Kanungo 2008).

Hindu and Pana Relationship

The emergence of Christian Panas and their possession of land, property and modern life aroused the anger of the Hindu trading community and their sponsored extremist groups. Particularly, after the liberalization of Indian economy in 1990s, this community started to open shops in different areas of Kandhamal. The educated youth took loans from banks and opened grocery and shops, emerging as the competitor to higher caste Hindu traders. A bitter relationship developed between these two groups of merchants. Moreover, higher caste shopkeepers started to link themselves with the Kandhas by giving them grocery commodities in credit and also they started to give loans to them. Gradually, people got polarized. Pana consumers sided with Pana merchants, and Kandha consumers went to higher caste Hindu. So competition in trade and commerce got overlaid by religion. This process got accentuated with political campaigns by religious leaders (Roul 2014).

Beginning of Manipulation by Extreme Forces

By extreme forces, we understand both VHP and Christian missionary. Both these forces understood the social, political and cultural equation of the above relationships between the major communities, involved in 2008 communal riot. By exploiting the social order (Kandhas and Panas coexistence) of Kandhamal, they started working towards their own agenda. This section of the chapter deals with the role of missionary and VHP in the manipulation process.

Role of Christian Missionary

The impact of organized activities of Christian missionaries on Kandha in the area began in 1894. Administrator J. Campbell was very anxious 'to see the penetration of Christian missionaries' (Pathy 1995: 227) in the region of Kandhamal. He pressed all officers for the expansion of roads and markets for the convenience of missionaries' arrival into the region. 'Several Christian missionaries infiltrated the area and started proselytizing and de-culturalising Kandhas. The first church was established at Digi in 1894 and the second was at Katingia' (Pathy 1995: 227). A Catholic church was established at Kanjamendi village in 1950. Due to the prohibition of *Meriah* practice by British government, Kandhas were dissatisfied with British administration and, hence, boycotted them in all possible forms. The missionaries got frustrated by this development and developed two alternative strategies: first, they made Pana community as their weapon to reach out the Kandha tribal. They provided all kinds of benefits to converted Panas for their upliftment. Second, they, through British administration, decided to organize markets where Kandha can congregate for daily uses, to get an opportunity to proselytize them. Hence, 'markets at different places of Kandha area established (Behera 1996: 69). In this way, weekly market (hata) was established in Kandhamal. Along with it, missionaries established schools for imparting education and knowledge of Christianity through the vernacular language (Pradhan 1985: 272). The seed of education was first planted in the Baliguda subdivision in 1851 by Captain Mac Viccar as par with the decision taken by Henry Pottinger in 1845 (Ratha 2006: 51). They opened *Meriah* school to educate *Meriah* who were rescued by them. In fact, missionaries immensely contributed for the social development of Kandhamal, but conversion was one of their goals.

The growing missionary activities in the social sector of Kandhamal put Kandhas in cultural and ethnic dilemma. Some Kandhas got converted and others disliked their conversion while perceiving it as the loss of their own identity, culture and society. Consequently, they established 'Nikhila Utkala Kui Samaj Union' in 1926 to preserve the dignity of Kui community. Similarly, 'Kui Seva Samiti' was formed in 1945 for the same purpose with only the membership of Kandhas (Roul 2014).

In postcolonial Kandhamal, church was the only active institution in religious matter. They followed the same methods of conversion that they were using in the colonial period. Along with it, specifically two new methods were adopted: harsh approach to Hinduism and political empowerment of converted Christians (Kanungo 2003). They started attack on Hinduism while strongly criticizing the philosophy of it with the allegation that this religion will not lead to salvation. They projected Christianity as the ultimate religion. Church wanted to make converted dalits politically empowered by which they can claim their due rights and entitlements. As a result, postcolonial Kandhamal politics saw increasing political assertion and power acquisition by Panas. They were quicker to pick up the idioms of this politics, its rule and benefits (Mohapatra and Bhattacharya 1996: 161).

Role of Hindutva Forces (VHP)

Politics of Hindutva is an important source of Kandha–Pana conflict in Kandhamal. The Hindutva activists understood the social equations in Kandhamal with the help of local higher caste people. They successfully convinced the tribal community that Panas are traitors, exploiters and grabbers of benefits meant for the tribals. They started to manipulate tribal issues in the name of religion and conversion. They inculcated the feelings among Kandhas through different ways that they too are Hindus. The nexus between the Sangh Parivar and the leaders of Adivasis came to light during the riots of 2008 (Roul 2014).

Along with it, Hindutva organization started manipulating demography to create a space to argue for its agenda. They raised a concern that the Christian population has risen to 18 per cent in the district compared to 8.7 per cent in 1991 census. The Sangh Parivar used the census data to raise alarm over conversions in Kandhamal by claiming that the Christian ratio has more than doubled between from 1991 to 2001. One of the important reasons for this eye-catching difference is the uneven demographic distribution resulting from the separation of Phulbani district in 1994. In the year 1991, the population of Christian community was 8.7 per cent in undivided Phulbani district. When this district was divided in the year 1994, demographically, 0.06 per cent of Christian came under Boudh district which in turn increased the Christian population to 18.1 per cent in Kandhamal. According to Parmar (2010: 12) 'there is a clear rise (from 8.7% to 11.5%) of 2.8% in Christian population; whereas decrease (from 91% to 88%) of 3% in Hindu population'. This increase of Christian population in Kandhamal may have resulted from many factors such as natural growth of population, migration of Christian families from outside, as well as outmigration of Hindus. One of the factors was also conversion. No one can deny fresh conversions in Kandhamal.

With the emergence of Swami Laxmanananda Saraswati in Kandhamal, real competitive religiosity started between Hindutva forces and Christian missionary on one hand, and Kandha and Pana on the other. Before this, it was just a unilateral or one-sided affair between Kandhas and Panas. The RSS functionaries realized that there is a necessity to counteract against the mass conversions by missionaries. They thought 'ideological challenge will not be enough unless tribals are Hinduized and an alternative welfare system is provided to woo them away from missionary welfare system' (Kanungo 2003). After achieving this, RSS thought 'to bring back the lost brothers to Hindu fold through re-conversion' (Kanungo 2003: 150).

Swami Laxmanananda Saraswati's religious activities were based on the notion of three cultures: Kandha tribe, Hinduism and Hindutva. He mainly adopted three methods to confront missionaries. These methods were campaign for *Ghar Wapsi* (home coming), *Gau Raksha Andolana* (campaign against cow slaughter) and *Paravartana* (reconversion). The *Ghar Wapsi* was with the purpose to bring back the Vanavasi Hindus who were 'lured' by the Christian missionaries (ibid.: 155). *Paravartana* was a programme, organized by the Ashram according to the rituals and customs laid down by *shastra*. The religious campaign of Swami had made many Kandha people vegetarian. They did not eat meat or fish and gave up drinking. They also wore sandal wood paste on their forehead and used saffron clothes to worship Hindu god. But they did not give up their tribal belief system. They wore the sacred thread like Brahmins. *Nama Sankritana* has spread in northern Kandhamal since the last three decades.

Mainly three strategies of cultural mobilization were undertaken by Hindutva forces: Firstly, *swadeshi* and *videshi* dichotomy; secondly, invention of tradition; and thirdly, policy of social ostracism. Christianity was said to be a foreign religion, not Indian, by the Hindutva forces. It was associated with British rule which had ruled Adivasis for several years. Moreover, Christians were equated with killers since adivasi leaders such as Birsa Munda and Laxman Nayak were killed under British rule. Along with it, Christians were said to be the exploiters of Kandha's resources by right-wing forces. On the other hand, these forces described Hinduism as *desi* religion, asking Kandhas to discover the traditions, culture, rites and rituals of Hinduism and Adivasis to counter the influence of Christianity. Kandhas were told by Hindutva forces that Hindu culture and traditions were very much connected with their history and culture. They said to Adivasis that, for them, Adivasis are '*vanabasis*' like lord Rama Chandra who had 14 years *vanwas* in his life. Lord Jagannath was made to be the link between Adivasis and Hindus in the sense that the priests at Jagannath temple were Adivasis by origin. They made the Adivasis understand that, for them, they were Hindu since Hindus are (Adi + Vasis) original residents. Right-wing forces did not accept that Adivasis are the original inhabitants of India and Aryans came from the outside (ibid.: 149). Policy of social ostracism was a very powerful strategy of cultural mobilization in the hand of Hindutva forces.

Conclusion

Conflict is happening everywhere in so many forms. Mostly conflict within the individual is very much related to his/her identity and social position. As long as identity prevails, conflict will continue to exist. Ideally, conflict demands/needs reconciliation/justice, but in reality, it gets manipulated by politics for its electoral success. This is what exactly happening in India and thereby Indian politics, in a sense, is known as 'communal politics'.

References

Bailey, F.G. 1960. *Tribe, Caste, Nation*, Bombay: Oxford University Press.

Behera, B.K. 1996. *Tribal's Culture, Modernization and Development: A Study of Kandha Tribe*, New Delhi: Khama Publishers.

'Kandhamal Lies Nailed', *Pioneer*, 22 July 2009.

Kanungo, Pralay. 2003. *RSS's Tryst with Politics: From Hedgewar to Sudarshan*, New Delhi: Manohar Publications.

Kanungo, Pralay. 2008. 'Hindutva's fury against Christians in Orissa', *Economic and Political Weekly*, Vol. 43, No. 37, pp. 16–19.

K.B. 2008. 'The Multi-Polar Truth of Kandhamal Conflict', *Mainstream*, Vol. XLVI, No. 46.

Kumar, Lenin. 2008. *Kandhamalre Dharma Naanre Raktara Nadi*, Bhubaneswar: Nisan.

Lingaraja. 2008. 'Kandhamal: Sampradayika-Jatikaran nian- Eka Bislesana', *Samadrusti*, Vol. 1, No. 15, pp. 35–7.

Mohapatra, Bishnu and D. Bhattacharya. 1996. 'Tribal-Dalit Conflict: Electoral Politics in Phulbani', *Economic and Political Weekly*, Vol. 31, Nos. 2/3, pp. 160–4.

Mohanty, N.R. 2008. 'Kandhamal: Issues and Challenges', *Seminar*, 591, pp. 61–65.

Mohanty, Sarat Chandra. 2008. 'Adivasi', *SCST RTI*, Vol. 48, No. 1.

Padel, Felix. 1995. *The Sacrifice of Human Being: British Rule and Khonds of Orissa*, New Delhi: Oxford University Press.

Parmar, Vijay. 2010. *Kandhamal in Chaos: An Account of Facts*, Ahmedabad: Jan Vikas.

Pathy, Jaganath. 1976. 'Political Economy of Kandhamal', *Men in India*, Vol. 56, No. 1, pp. 1–36.

Pathy, Jaganath. 1995. 'Colonial Ethnography of the Kondha: 'White men's Burden' or Political Expediency?', *Economic and Political Weekly*, Vol. 30, No. 4, pp. 220–8.

Pati, Biswamoy. 2001. 'Identity, Hegemony, Resistance: Conversion in Orissa, 1800–2000', *Economic and Political Weekly*, Vol. 36, No. 44, pp. 4204–12.

Pradhan, A.C. 1985. *A Study of the History of Orissa*, Bhubaneswar: Pancasila.

Ratha, Raghunath. 1993. *Kandha Sanskrutira Analochita Adhyaya*, Koraput: Satta Sahitya Sansad.

Ratha, Raghunath. 2006. 'Education of Tribal Children in Kandhamal District', *Orissa Review*, May, pp. 50–9.

Ratha, Raghunath. 2010. *The Kandhas and Kandhamal*, Bhubaneswar: Amadeus Press.

Roul, Kamalakanta. 2014. *Kandhamal Violence and the State: A Study of Politics of Ethnicity, Caste, Class and Politics*, PhD Thesis, New Delhi: Delhi University.

Russell, R.V. and Hiralal. 1916. *The Tribes and Castes of the Central Province of India, Vol. III*, California: University of California Libraries.

Schulze, F.V.P. 1911. *Kuvi Grammar*, Madras.

Senapati, Nilamani, and Durga Charan Kunar. 1980. Orissa District Gazetteer, Bouda Kandhamal. Cuttack.

Swaro, Dasarathi. 1990. *The Christian Missionaries in Orissa: Their impact on Nineteenth Century Society*, Calcutta: Punthi Pustaka.

Thiady, S. 1965. *Phulbani the Khond Land*, Berhampur: Arun Press.

Winfield, W.W. 1929. *A Vocabulary of Kui Language*, Calcutta: Asiatic Society of Bengal.

Index